THE LOOK BOOK

First published in 2011 by Zest Books
35 Stillman Street, Suite 121, San Francisco, CA 94107
www.zestbooks.net
Created and produced by Zest Books, San Francisco, CA

© 2011 by Zest Books LLC

Typeset in Adobe Jenson Pro and Futura; Title text set in CoffeeShop
Teen Nonfiction / Beauty

Library of Congress Control Number: 2010936582

ISBN-13: 978-0-9819733-8-8
ISBN-10: 0-9819733-8-8

CREDITS
EDITORIAL DIRECTOR/BOOK EDITOR: Karen Macklin
CREATIVE DIRECTOR: Hallie Warshaw
ART DIRECTOR/COVER DESIGN: Tanya Napier
ILLUSTRATOR: Ana Carolina Pesce
PHOTO EDITOR: Nikki Roddy
MANAGING and PRODUCTION EDITOR: Pam McElroy
RESEARCH ASSISTANTS: Ann Edwards and Megan Fischer-Prins

TEEN ADVISORS: Emma Herlihy, Celina Reynes, Diana Rae Valenzuela, Irene Xu

Manufactured in China
LEO 10 9 8 7 6 5 4 3 2 1
4500276296

Every effort has been made to ensure that the information presented is accurate. The publisher disclaims any liability for injuries, losses, untoward results, or any other damages that may result from the use of the information in this book.

All photos courtesy of Photofest with the exception of Aishwarya Rai Bachchan (page 48), Iman (page 78), and Björk (page 82), which are courtesy of Getty Images.

THE LOOK BOOK

50 ICONIC BEAUTIES AND HOW
TO ACHIEVE THEIR SIGNATURE STYLES

By Erika Stalder

With celebrity hair and makeup artists Christopher Fulton and Cameron Cohen

INTRODUCTION

People often just see the picture-perfect hair and faces of celebrities but don't know the story behind their famous looks. For instance, Coco Chanel was able to bring the tan into fashion only after the poor had become pale from working indoors during the industrial revolution. And Iman became the queen of foundation because no one else at the time was making appropriate makeup for women with her skin tone. And did you know that film director Roman Polanski's decision to chop off Mia Farrow's locks wound up making a huge feminist statement? Or that Veronica Lake's famed peek-a-boo curl was a result of a hair accident that happened while she was shooting a film?

Beauty icons and their looks are made famous by a combination of natural beauty, personal drive, and being in the right place at the right time with the right makeup artists, film directors, glossy-magazine editors, publicists, and dedicated fan base. In this book, you'll meet 50 of the most influential women in beauty history, from Marilyn Monroe to Twiggy, and learn about their lives and how their famous looks came into being. Even better, you'll learn how to get their signature looks for yourself by following the user-friendly instructions provided by two of today's celebrity hair and makeup pros.

Ever wonder how to get your hair as straight as Naomi Campbell's? Curious about how to achieve Kate Winslet's no-makeup makeup? Want to get Kat Von D's face tattoos—without actually getting a tattoo? *The Look Book* will show you step-by-step.

And don't think you always have to wear the iconic looks exactly as they are presented here. Many of the icons in this book were beauty innovators themselves, dissatisfied by the techniques and styles that already existed and wanting to create something entirely new. So, once you get your technique down, start experimenting. Develop your own special spin on a look, or combine two or three looks together. With a little bit of knowledge of beauty history and the basic tools of the trade, you too can create the next big look. And—if the stars align—you may even become a beauty icon in your own right.

CONTENTS

BRUSH UP ON

Sure, most makeup can be slapped on with a finger or two. But when it comes to executing the perfectly rouged cheek versus looking like you got punched in the face, using the right tools can make all the difference. Because there is a huge selection of makeup brushes specially created for different jobs, identifying each type of brush and knowing when to use the right one can leave a beauty maven bewildered. Here's a cheatsheet for the basic types of makeup brushes and what they're most commonly used for.

POWDER BRUSH: used to apply and blend face powder

ANGLED EYELINER BRUSH: used to apply eyeliner

LIP BRUSH: used to apply and blend lipsticks and glosses

CONCEALER BRUSH: used to apply and blend concealer

EYE SHADOW FLUFF BRUSH: used to apply and blend base layers of eye shadow

WEDGE SPONGE: used to apply and blend foundation

YOUR BRUSHES

PRO TIP

Clean brushes after you use them with warm water and a touch of shampoo, and lay flat to dry. This will sustain the lifespan of your brushes and ensure you won't inadvertently mar today's look with a hint of yesterday's makeup.

SMUDGE BRUSH:
used to apply secondary layers of eye shadow and to blend eyeliner and eye shadow

ANGLED BROW BRUSH:
used to apply eye shadow to the brows

BLUSH BRUSH:
used to apply and blend blush to the apples of the cheeks

ANGLED BLUSH BRUSH:
used to apply and blend blush to create definition

SPOOLIE BRUSH:
used to apply mascara and groom brows

CREASE BRUSH:
used to apply and blend eye shadow at the crease

FINE POINTED LINER BRUSH:
used to apply eyeliner and draw faux lashes and tattoos

LIPS

When it comes to makeup, lipstick is the easiest, and quickest way to make a statement. User friendly and ready to wear, lipstick allows us to add color to our faces with just a few simple strokes. In a matter of seconds, we can take our pout from plain to juicy red (Marilyn Monroe, page 22) or sweet and glossy (Christie Brinkley, page 26). But wearing lip color wasn't always socially acceptable; in fact, lipstick used to be primarily worn by prostitutes! Celebrities helped to turn this idea around in the early 1900s, when stars like Sarah Bernhardt, Clara Bow (page 12), and Louise Brooks wore crimson lips on film. Soon, the bad-girl stigma that surrounded lipstick was lifted and everyday gals started sporting their own colorful lips. Today, beauty icons of all kinds make their lips the centerpiece of their looks—and you can, too!

CLARA BOW (1905 – 1965)

In the 1920s, young American women had just won the right to vote, and were also asserting themselves by hanging out in jazz bars and wearing short, flirty flapper dresses that publicly exposed their bare legs like never before. It was the perfect time for the debut of film star and party girl Clara Bow. Clara made more than 50 films, but it was her movie *It* (1927), in which she played a sexy and conniving shop girl, that made her an icon of the flapper generation and America's first "It Girl." The movie title referred to sex appeal, and Bow had "It" in spades.

On screen and off, Clara wore her signature Cupid's bow—or bee-stung—lips. To achieve this look, which was originated by Hollywood makeup artist Max Factor, lip color was applied to the center of the lips and then blended outward. The technique was initially developed to solve the problem of actress' pomade-based lip color running into the corners of their mouths and bleeding into their foundation. But the heart-shaped look that resulted became the new fashion.

Clara's rise to fame coincided with the burgeoning makeup industry's release of red lipstick to the public. For the first time, American women had the proper tools to paint on the flirty red lips that had only been seen in movies. And it was Clara who inspired them to do it.

Essential Clara

- *It* (film, 1927)
- *Clara Bow: Runnin' Wild* (biography, 2000)
- *The Actors: Rare Films of Clara Bow* (movie collection DVD, 2009)

> **"**We did as we pleased. We stayed up late. We dressed the way we wanted. I'd whiz down Sunset Boulevard in my open-air Kissel with seven red chow dogs to match my hair.**"**
>
> —Clara Bow

CUPID'S BOW LIPS

WORKS BEST ON

Anyone

TOOLS NEEDED

- Dry toothbrush
- Deep red lip liner pencil (darker than the lipstick)
- Lip brush
- Red lipstick
- Tissue
- Powder brush
- Translucent powder (loose or pressed)

TIME IT TAKES

4 minutes

HOW TO DO IT

❶ With the dry toothbrush, exfoliate your lips by gently brushing them and removing any dry or chapped skin.

❷ With the lip liner pencil, line your bottom lip. Start at the center of your lip line and follow your lip line out to the corners. At about 2/3 of the way to the corners, draw the line upward, across your lip at a 45-degree angle, leaving the corners of your mouth unlined.

❸ Line your top lip with a lip pencil by starting in the center and moving outward, following the peaks of the lips. (To exaggerate the Cupid's bow, draw slightly outside your natural lip line—this will create the illusion of a fuller lip.) After drawing the peaks, follow your natural lip line again for about 1/3 of the way to the corner, and then draw the line downward across the lip at a 45-degree angle to meet the endpoint of the bottom lip line.

❹ Dab a bit of red lipstick onto the lip brush, and apply the color to the surface area of your lip, staying within the lines you have created. Slightly blend the lipstick into the liner with the brush.

❺ Place a tissue over your lips. With your powder brush, lightly dust a bit of translucent powder onto the tissue in the area that covers your lips. (Using this technique will set your lipstick, and prevent you from getting powder all over your face and from getting lipstick on your powder brush.) Remove the tissue.

❻ Apply a final layer of lipstick to both lips. When finished, do not rub your lips together—it will mess up your perfectly drawn line. If you need to touch up your lips later on, simply reapply the lipstick instead of wiping it all away and starting over.

Also Seen On

Molly Ringwald

Betty Boop

Lady Gaga

Jacqueline (Jackie) Bouvier Kennedy Onassis is known for a life of tremendous variety: She was a first lady to President John F. Kennedy, a book editor, a fashion icon, a historical preservationist, a wife to a Greek shipping tycoon, and a paparazzi magnet. But despite the number of roles she played throughout her life, one thing stayed consistent—her petal-soft makeup and effortless beauty.

Jackie never wore a heavily painted face or bold and trendy colors. Her look simply complemented her features and radiated classic American beauty. Whether being photographed as first lady, vacationing in Capri, or attending a black-tie gala, Jackie was never without her brown eyeliner, velvet pink blush, and sheer pink lipstick that sparkled with a hint of frost. So inspiring was Jackie's look that makeup companies went on to produce Jackie-inspired pink lipsticks, and even entire cosmetic lines, to mimic it. One such line was issued in 2001 by Prescriptives and sold out immediately after its release—even four decades after Jackie was sworn in as first lady, women were still clamoring to look like her.

"You have to be doing something you enjoy. That is a definition of happiness: Complete use of one's faculties along lines leading to excellence in a life affording them scope. It applies to women as well as to men. We can't all reach it, but we can try to reach it to some degree.**"**

—Jackie Kennedy

Essential Jackie

- *Jacqueline Kennedy Onassis: In a Class of Her Own* (documentary, 1996)
- *Jackie Style* (biography, 2001)
- *The Jackie Handbook* (biography, 2005)

FROSTED PINK LIPS

WORKS BEST ON
Anyone

TOOLS NEEDED
- Dry toothbrush
- Light pink lip liner
- Clear lip gloss
- Light shimmery pink lipstick (glitter free)

TIME IT TAKES
2 minutes

HOW TO DO IT

❶ With the dry toothbrush, exfoliate your lips by gently brushing them and removing any dry or chapped skin.

❷ With the lip liner pencil, line your bottom lip. Start at the center of your lip line and follow your lip line out to the corners.

❸ Line your top lip. Start in the center of your lip and follow the peaks, making them rounded and not pointed. After drawing the peaks, follow your lip line down to the corners.

❹ Apply the lipstick to the surface area of your lip, staying within the lines you have created.

❺ To add an additional dimension of shine, add a touch of clear gloss (just a little to ensure you don't take away the shimmer in the lipstick). When finished, do not rub your lips together—it will mess up your perfectly drawn line. If you need to touch up your lips later on, simply reapply the lipstick instead of wiping it all away and starting over.

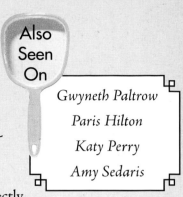

Also Seen On

Gwyneth Paltrow

Paris Hilton

Katy Perry

Amy Sedaris

PRO TIP

To achieve a classic look, pair frosted pink lips with a soft pink blush (see pages 87 and 89) and a winged eye (see page 31). Light pink is considered a neutral lip color and goes with anything you wear.

PRO TIP

To figure out which shade of pink lipstick is right for your skin tone, use the guide below. A makeup pro can help you, as well.

Skin Tone	Best Shade of Pink
Pale	Magenta, fuchsia
Medium	Pale pink, berry
Dark brown	Bubble gum, coral

JEAN SHRIMPTON (1942 –)

Jean "the shrimp" Shrimpton emerged as a supermodel in 1960s London during a time when the full skirts and bouffant hair of the '50s were being replaced with edgy new trends like mini-skirts and geometric haircuts. Jean had the looks to become a successful model on her own, but her relationship with seminal fashion photographer David Bailey, from 1960 to 1964, was a huge boon to her career. During that time, the pair produced Jean's signature look and hundreds of profile-raising pictures together. Jean became known as the "Face of the '60s," was named *Glamour* magazine's Model of the Year in 1963, and went on to appear on the cover of *Vogue* 19 times throughout her career.

Jean had a unique look, but it was her pale pout that was revolutionary: It was painted so white that it all but disappeared from her face. (Sometimes the look was topped with faint lip color.) Her lips became known as quintessentially Mod, a style-obsessed, youth-centric subculture that encouraged women to look modern and trendy. Before this time, lip color was strictly used to create a look that was dark and sensual (Lauren Bacall, page 20) or juicy and sexy (Marilyn Monroe, page 22), or to play up the perfect pink pucker (Jackie Kennedy, page 14). Jean influenced everyone—from young things in London to hippie chicks in California—to take a stab at edgy beauty.

Essential Jean

- *My Own Story: The Truth About Modeling* (autobiography, 1965)

- *Privilege* (film, 1967)

- *Jean Shrimpton: An Autobiography* (autobiography, 1992)

- *Fame, Fashion and Photography: The Real Blow Up* (documentary, 2002)

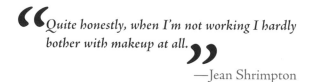

Quite honestly, when I'm not working I hardly bother with makeup at all.

—Jean Shrimpton

PALE LIPS

WORKS BEST ON
Anyone

TOOLS NEEDED
- Dry toothbrush
- Liquid foundation
- Powder brush
- Translucent powder (loose or pressed)
- Light pink lip liner
- Light pink lipstick
- Clear lip gloss

TIME IT TAKES
2 minutes

HOW TO DO IT

❶ With the dry toothbrush, exfoliate your lips by gently brushing them and removing any dry or chapped skin.

❷ With a finger, evenly apply a bit of foundation to the entire surface of your lips.

❸ With the powder brush, dust some of the translucent powder on your lips. (The foundation and powder will create a neutral base for the light pink lip color.)

❹ With the lip liner pencil, line your bottom lip. Start at the center of your lip line and follow your lip line out to the corners.

❺ Line your top lip. Start in the center of your lip and follow the peaks, making them rounded and not pointed. After drawing the peaks, follow your lip line down to the corners.

Also Seen On

Mary Quant
Julie Christie
Brigitte Bardot

❻ Apply the lipstick to the surface area of your lip, staying within the lines you have created.

❼ Add a touch of clear gloss to just the center of both lips to make them appear fuller. When finished, do not rub your lips together—it will mess up your perfectly drawn line. If you need to touch up your lips later on, simply reapply the lipstick instead of wiping it all away and starting over.

JOAN CRAWFORD (1905 – 1977)

A highly acclaimed film star, Joan Crawford was most famously known for her depictions of temperamental and hysterical women in legendary films such as *Whatever Happened to Baby Jane?* (1962) and *Torch Song* (1953). But aside from being remembered for her portrayals of prima donnas, she can also be thought of as something of a pre-Madonna: She was the original style-setting chameleon of the beauty world.

When Joan arrived in Hollywood in the 1920s, she immediately tamed her frizzy hair and used heavy makeup to hide her natural freckles and meet the beauty standards of the time. She also practiced obsessive beauty rituals like rubbing ice cubes on her skin to minimize pores and reportedly had some of her back teeth removed in an effort to create more defined cheekbones.

In the '30s, at Joan's request, Hollywood makeup legend Max Factor created The Smear—or Hunter's bow—lipstick look.

This look was achieved by painting outside the natural lip line to create huge lips that didn't peak in the middle. The Smear was a bold, sultry, and pouty look that was unusual, inventive, and perfectly Joan Crawford. But Joan was never one to cling to a signature style. Over her career, she repeatedly changed up her look to stay ahead of the curve.

Essential Joan

- *The Women* (film, 1939)
- *Mildred Pierce* (film, 1945)
- *Whatever Happened to Baby Jane?* (film, 1962)
- *My Way of Life* (autobiography, 1972)

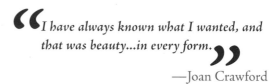

I have always known what I wanted, and that was beauty...in every form.

—Joan Crawford

SMEAR LIPS

WORKS BEST ON
Anyone

TOOLS NEEDED
- Dry toothbrush
- Wedge sponge
- Foundation
- Powder brush
- Loose powder
- Lip pencil (a color very close to that of the lipstick)
- Lip brush
- Lipstick (a bold color, like red or orange)

TIME IT TAKES
4 minutes

HOW TO DO IT

❶ With the dry toothbrush, exfoliate your lips by gently brushing them and removing any dry or chapped skin.

❷ With the wedge sponge, evenly apply a thin layer of foundation to the surface of your lips to set a neutral-colored base, and to camouflage the peaks of the top lip.

❸ Dab a bit of loose powder onto the powder brush and tap the brush to release any excess. Then lightly dust the surface of your lips to set the foundation.

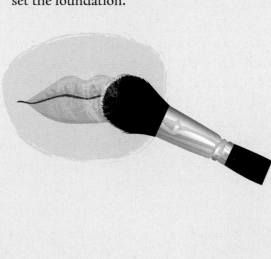

❹ With the lip liner pencil, line your bottom lip. Start at the center of your lip line and draw an exaggerated line out to the corners that will create a slightly fuller lip.

Also Seen On

Lucille Ball
Oprah
Rita Hayworth

❺ Line your top lip. Start at the center of your lip. Rather than exaggerate the natural peaks of the lip line, minimize them by drawing only slight, barely noticeable curves across the peaks. Then continue with the exaggerated line out toward the corners to create a fuller lip at the sides.

❻ Dab a bit of lipstick onto the lip brush, and then use it to fill in the surface of the lip. When finished, do not rub your lips together—it will mess up your perfectly drawn line. If you need to touch up your lips later on, simply reapply the lipstick instead of wiping it all away and starting over.

PRO TIP

For an even bolder look, fill your lips in with the lip liner after Step 4, before applying the lipstick. A base coat of lip liner can also help the lipstick stay vibrant longer.

LAUREN BACALL (1924 –)

Silver screen star Lauren Bacall first entered the public eye in 1943 as a 19-year-old *Harper's Bazaar* model. Hollywood execs saw the photos of the dark-haired girl with the dramatic V-shaped brows, heavy lids, long lashes, and seductive gaze (which later earned her the nickname "The Look"), and immediately put her in films.

Unlike many of the bottle-bleached blondes of the time who played wide-eyed ingénues on screen, Lauren had rich mahogany tresses and took parts as sophisticated characters like chanteuse Marie "Slim" Browning in *To Have and Have Not* (1944) and clothing designer Marilla Brown in *Designing Woman* (1957). Because of her darker look and seriousness as an actress, she became known as the "thinking man's" sex symbol.

Lauren was famous for her deep, whisky-tinged voice, and a full, darkly painted mouth that looked just as velvety as the voice behind it. Her allure captivated her audiences and her costars, like dapper leading man Humphrey "Bogie" Bogart, whom she famously married after they met on the set of *To Have and Have Not*. "Bogie and Bacall," as the pair was known, made three more movies together in the next four years and became the most talked-about Hollywood couple. And women who aspired to Lauren's sexy, intelligent mystique painted on dark lips of their own, making Lauren's lips legendary.

Essential Lauren

- *To Have and Have Not* (film, 1944)

- *How to Marry a Millionaire* (film, 1953)

- *Sex and the Single Girl* (film, 1964)

- *Lauren Bacall: By Myself* (autobiography, 1985)

- *The Mirror Has Two Faces* (film, 1996)

VELVET LIPS

WORKS BEST ON
Anyone

TOOLS NEEDED
- Dry toothbrush
- Concealer
- Raisin-colored lip liner pencil (freshly sharpened)
- Raisin-colored lipstick
- Lip brush
- Tissue
- Powder brush
- Translucent powder (loose or pressed)

TIME IT TAKES
2 minutes

HOW TO DO IT

❶ With the dry toothbrush, exfoliate your lips by gently brushing them and removing any dry or chapped skin.

❷ To create a neutral base for the lip color, dab a bit of concealer onto your finger and lightly tap the surface of the entire lip with product.

❸ With the lip liner pencil, line your bottom lip. Start at the center of your lip line and follow your lip line out to the corners.

❹ Line your top lip. Start in the center of your lip and follow the peaks, making them rounded and not pointed. After drawing the peaks, follow your lip line down to the corners.

❺ Apply the lipstick to the surface area of your lip, staying within the lines you have created. Blend the lipstick into the liner using a lip brush.

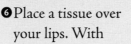

Also Seen On

Winona Ryder
Angelina Jolie
Dita Von Teese

❻ Place a tissue over your lips. With the powder brush, lightly dust a bit of translucent powder onto the tissue in the area that covers your lips. (Using this technique will set the lipstick, and prevent you from getting powder all over your face and from getting lipstick on the powder brush.) Remove the tissue.

❼ Apply a final layer of lipstick to your lips. When finished, do not rub your lips together—it will mess up your perfectly drawn line. If you need to touch up your lips later on, simply reapply the lipstick instead of wiping it all away and starting over.

PRO TIP

To create a more defined lip line, and to prevent the lipstick from bleeding, dab a bit of concealer onto the edges of your top and bottom lips with the concealer brush when finished.

> *I used to tremble from nerves so badly that the only way I could hold my head steady was to lower my chin practically to my chest and look up at Bogie. That was the beginning of 'The Look'.*
>
> —Lauren Bacall

MARILYN MONROE (1926 – 1962)

One of the most famous beauty icons of all time, Marilyn Monroe was the epitome of glamour. Her roles in movies like *Gentlemen Prefer Blondes* (1953) and *How to Marry A Millionaire* (1953), and her rumored affairs with the Kennedy brothers, gave her unprecedented siren status in Hollywood history. She became well known for her revealing dresses and bleach blonde hair, and when it came to makeup, she was the ultimate red-lipstick girl.

It's not that Marilyn was the first woman to don bright-red lips—the trend started years before (in fact, in 1912, makeup maven Elizabeth Arden gave every woman who marched for equal rights in New York City a stick of red lipstick to wear as a symbol of power). But Marilyn redefined red lips by the way she wore them: with unsurpassed sex appeal. She often posed for pictures with her red lips seductively parted, something that was considered quite racy for the time.

Essential Marilyn

- *The Seven Year Itch* (film, 1955)
- *Bus Stop* (film, 1956)
- *Some Like It Hot* (film, 1959)
- *My Story* (autobiography, 2006)
- *Marilyn Monroe: The Complete Last Sitting* (photo book, 2006)

While Marilyn made it look easy, she privately had to work at transforming her bare face to what the public expected to see. It reportedly took the star three hours to achieve her look, which consisted of flicked cat-eye makeup (see page 51), flawless skin (achieved by applying layer after layer of Vaseline and powder), and her iconic candy-apple lips.

> **"***Hollywood's a place where they'll pay you a thousand dollars for a kiss, and fifty cents for your soul. I know, because I turned down the first offer often enough and held out for the fifty.***"**
>
> —Marilyn Monroe

JUICY, RED LIPS

WORKS BEST ON
Anyone

TOOLS NEEDED
- Dry toothbrush
- Red lip liner pencil
- Red lipstick
- Tissue
- Translucent powder (loose or pressed)
- Powder brush

TIME IT TAKES
5 minutes

HOW TO DO IT

❶ With the dry toothbrush, exfoliate your lips by gently brushing them and removing any dry or chapped skin.

❷ With the lip liner pencil, line your bottom lip. Start at the center of your lip line and follow your lip line out to the corners.

❸ Line your top lip. Start in the center of your lip and follow the peaks, making them rounded and not pointed. After drawing the peaks, follow your lip line down to the corners.

❹ Fill in your lips with the same lip liner pencil.

❺ Apply the lipstick to the surface area of your lip, staying within the lines you have created.

❻ Place a tissue over your lips. With the powder brush, lightly dust a bit of translucent powder onto the tissue in the area that covers your lips. (Using this technique will set the lipstick, and prevent you from getting powder all over your face and from getting lipstick on the powder brush.) Remove the tissue.

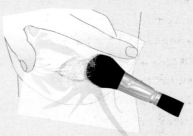

❼ Apply a final layer of lipstick (this will make your lips look wet). When finished, do not rub your lips together—it will mess up your perfectly drawn line. If you need to touch up your lips later on, simply reapply the lipstick instead of wiping it all away and starting over.

PRO TIP

To figure out which shade of red lipstick is right for your skin tone, use the guide below. A makeup pro can help you, as well.

Skin Tone	Best Shade of Red
Pale	Plum, wine, blue-red
Medium	Rose, mauve, berry
Dark brown	Pinkish, fuchsia, poppy

CATHERINE DENEUVE (1943 –)

Catherine Deneuve has starred in more than 100 films, and has garnered a reputation as being one of the greatest actresses of her generation. She's also enjoyed a somewhat unintentional second career as a beauty icon. She was chosen as the face of Chanel in the '70s, deemed France's "Marianne" (a rare title that is given to a woman who represents the country's values) in 1985, and also represented makeup company MAC in the 2000s.

One might think a beauty of this caliber might don a ton of makeup, but Catherine never has. She's known for her quick and breezy makeup routine, and even went completely makeup-free for her English-language film debut, *Repulsion* (1965). Two years later, her role as Séverine in the film *Belle de Jour* cemented her natural, yet sexy iconic image. She played a housewife who secretly doubled as a call girl, and donned a seductive trench coat along with her now famous cool, beige lips.

Off-screen, Catherine's style has continued to be influenced by Séverine's and that same nude lipstick has become her signature look. The image she created has had a lasting impression, not only on the public, but also on the makeup industry: In 1994, makeup guru François Nars created a sheer beige lipstick color in homage to her called "Belle de Jour."

Essential Catherine

- *Repulsion* (film, 1965)
- *Belle de Jour* (film, 1967)
- *Indochine* (film, 1992)
- *Dancer in the Dark* (film, 2000)
- *The Private Diaries of Catherine Deneuve: Close Up and Personal* (autobiography, 2007)

> "*I know that if I didn't look the way I looked, I would never have started in films. That, I remember, and I know I have to accept it.*"
>
> —Catherine Deneuve

NUDE LIPS

WORKS BEST ON
Darker skin tones

TOOLS NEEDED
- Dry toothbrush
- Nude lip liner (slightly darker than the lipstick)
- Nude lipstick
- Clear lip gloss

TIME IT TAKES
2 minutes

HOW TO DO IT

❶ With the dry toothbrush, exfoliate your lips by gently brushing them and removing any dry or chapped skin.

❷ With the lip liner pencil, line your bottom lip. Start at the center of your lip line and follow your lip line out to the corners.

❸ Line your top lip. Start in the center of your lip and follow the peaks, making them rounded and not pointed. After drawing the peaks, follow your lip line down to the corners.

❹ With the lip liner pencil, fill in the four corners of your lips so that, if you hold your index finger up to your lips like you're shushing someone, that center area of your lip that your finger covers is left bare.

❺ Generously cover the entire surface area of your lips with nude lipstick.

❻ Add a touch of gloss to the center of your lips to magnify fullness. When finished, do not rub your lips together—it will mess up your perfectly drawn line. If you need to touch up your lips later on, simply reapply the lipstick instead of wiping it all away and starting over.

Also Seen On

Julie Christie
Jennifer Lopez
Eve
Diane Kruger

CHRISTIE BRINKLEY (1954 –)

The late 1970s marked the end of an era that included the Vietnam War, the sexual revolution, and the rise of hippie counterculture. After two decades of chaos, many Americans were eager to embrace conservative values—and a more conservative style of beauty. Enter wholesome supermodel Christie Brinkley.

With her blonde hair, slightly bronzed skin, pug nose, and blue eyes, Christie embodied 1980s-style American beauty. A southern California native and former surfer, Christie became famous for her athletic build and ultra-glossy, high-wattage smile. She not only looked the part of the healthy, all-American good girl, she played the part too: While many models were taking drugs and staying out late, Christie kept her distance from the party scene. The countless images of Christie bestowed on the public showed her cheerfully embodying the go-getter spirit that characterized the Reagan era.

Christie soon secured a lucrative contract with CoverGirl cosmetics, and went on to represent the company in print and TV ads for 20 years, the longest contract a model has ever had with a cosmetics company. Christie did occasionally deviate from her wholesome persona (she was a three-time cover model for the *Sports Illustrated* swimsuit issue), but

she always kept it clean. Even when posing for the notoriously racy *Playboy* magazine, Christie kept her private parts tastefully concealed, so as not to tarnish her image.

Essential Christie

- *Sports Illustrated* swimsuit issue cover (1979, 1980, 1981)
- *Vacation* (film, 1983)
- "Uptown Girl" (Billy Joel music video, 1983)

> *Number one, you have to take care of yourself, and that means eating right, living a healthy lifestyle. That really does do wonders for you.*
>
> —Christie Brinkley

GLOSSY LIPS

WORKS BEST ON
Anyone

TOOLS NEEDED
- Dry toothbrush
- Lip gloss (any color)
- Lip pencil (in the same shade as the lip gloss)
- Lip brush (optional)

TIME IT TAKES
3 minutes

HOW TO DO IT

❶ With the dry toothbrush, exfoliate your lips by gently brushing them and removing any dry or chapped skin.

❷ With the lip liner pencil, line your bottom lip. Start at the center of your lip line and follow your lip line out to the corners.

❸ Line your top lip. Start in the center of your lip and follow the peaks, making them rounded and not pointed. After drawing the peaks, follow your lip line down to the corners.

❹ Using a lip brush or your finger, cover your lips generously with lip gloss to give them a soft, wet look.

Also Seen On

Michelle Pfeiffer
Dakota Fanning
Drew Barrymore
Blake Lively

PRO TIP

Lip gloss makes lips glisten, look bigger, and show up better in photos, so wear as much of it as possible when you know you'll be photographed.

PRO TIP
To determine what lip color is best for you, examine the undertones in your skin. If you have cool undertones (your cheeks are red or slightly ruddy), wear a cool color. If you have warm undertones (your cheeks are golden or sallow), wear a warm color.

EYES

People say the eyes are the window to the soul, so it's no surprise that we love to draw attention to them. And women have been decorating their eyes for ages—since the days of Ancient Egypt! No matter what your mood, eye makeup can help you express it. Want to look mysterious? Try a smoky eye, like Joan Jett (page 44). Want to look bright-eyed and curious? Go Audrey Hepburn-style and draw a winged eye (page 30). To be innocent and sweet, you can imitate Twiggy's Kewpie doll lashes (page 42). Or channel Edie Sedgwick's raccoon eyes (page 32) for that tough-as-nails look. There's really no limit to the moods you can create with just a bit of eye shadow, mascara, and liner. So learn the eye makeup of the stars, and find a whole new meaning in giving someone "the eye."

AUDREY HEPBURN (1929 – 1993)

Audrey Hepburn is known as one of Hollywood's all-time great beauties. A delicate girl, Audrey was known for her captivating smile, cropped dark hair and slight, boyish figure—a look that contrasted with that of her curvy blonde contemporaries like Marilyn Monroe. But even though Audrey's look was considered unconventional, that didn't stop her from winning the hearts of American audiences.

Audrey will always be remembered for her portrayal of New York City party girl Holly Golightly in the 1961 film *Breakfast at Tiffany's*. But it was her first major (and Oscar-winning) role in the 1953 film *Roman Holiday* that established her as a beauty icon. She played the part of a bored, adventure-seeking princess who starts hanging out with a journalist (played by Gregory Peck) in Rome. She famously wore strong brows and eyeliner that was drawn out and up past the outer corner of her eye in the shape of a small wing. Women everywhere started to emulate her look, and still do. In fact, it's rare that you hear the term "winged eye" without hearing a mention of the famed Audrey.

> *I never thought I'd land pictures with a face like mine.*
> —Audrey Hepburn

Essential Audrey

- *Roman Holiday* (film, 1953)
- *Sabrina* (film, 1954)
- *Breakfast at Tiffany's* (film, 1961)
- *Audrey Style* (biography, 1999)
- *Fifth Avenue, 5 A.M.* (book on *Breakfast at Tiffany's*, 2010)

WINGED EYES

WORKS BEST ON

Anyone

TOOLS NEEDED

- Angled eyeliner brush
- Black indelible gel eyeliner
- Eyelash curler (optional, see Pro Tip)
- Black mascara (optional, see Pro Tip)
- Dry toothbrush (optional, see Pro Tip)

TIME IT TAKES

10 minutes

HOW TO DO IT

❶ Tilt your head back a bit so that when you are looking in the mirror, it feels like you are looking down on your reflection. (This way, you can see what you are doing while applying the liner without having to blink. This also keeps your eyelid smooth; a closed eye becomes too wrinkled to apply liner.)

❷ Lightly sweep the angled eyeliner brush across the surface of the eyeliner gel, being sure to pick up liner on both sides of the brush. Then, draw a thin to medium line along your upper lash line, starting in the center of your

eyelid and moving out to the outside corner of your eye. When you reach the corner, pull the line straight out and upward a little past the corner of your eye to create a "wing." (This will open up your eye instead of making it droop.)

Also Seen On

Nicole Richie
Lauren Conrad
Brigitte Bardot
Alexa Chung

❸ Take the eyeliner brush (reapply liner gel if needed) to the center of your upper eyelid where you started your line in Step 2. Now, draw a thin line along the upper lash line to the inside corner of your eye to complete the look.

PRO TIP

To accentuate the winged eye look, you can also curl your lashes with a lash curler and then apply a generous coat of mascara, pulling the outer lashes toward your ear with the mascara wand. To prevent clumping, take a flat, dry toothbrush and brush your lashes while the mascara is still wet.

PRO TIP

Be sure to clean your brush after every use—liquid liner will ruin the brush if it's left on to dry. Also, close the liner container completely when you're done. Any air leak will dry the liner and make it too hard to use.

EDIE SEDGWICK (1943 – 1971)

EYES

When California native and career party girl Edie Sedgwick arrived in New York City in 1964, she became an instant addition to pop artist Andy Warhol's handpicked clique of beautiful and eccentric muses. Edie's avant-garde style was twisted and irreverent, and totally in line with the experimental Mod fashion movement that was happening in London. She often wore long T-shirts with tights (setting a fashion template for future stars like the Olsen twins and Lady Gaga). And when it came to makeup, she sported dark thick brows, heavy black raccoon eyes, false lashes (see page 39), and very little else on her pale, pale face.

Edie's eye makeup wasn't anything new—silent film star Theda Bara was the first to give the raccoon eye look a national spotlight after starring in a vampire flick called *The Stain* in 1914. But Edie brought the look into the mainstream, and inspired party girls—and future party girls—to wear it themselves.

Sadly, Edie's fame faded away just as quickly as it had come: She died of a drug overdose in 1971. But despite her meteoric rise and fall in the public eye, her dark, dramatic eye makeup made an indelible impression on beauty culture, and remains a style staple in the Goth and club-kid subcultures of today.

Also Seen On

Lindsay Lohan
Taylor Momsen
Elizabeth Jagger

> **"**I made a mask out of my face because I didn't realize I was quite beautiful.**"**
> —Edie Sedgwick

Essential Edie

- *Poor Little Rich Girl* (film, 1965)
- *Edie: American Girl* (biography, 1994)
- *Factory Girl* (biopic, 2006)

RACCOON EYES

WORKS BEST ON
Anyone

TOOLS NEEDED

- Eye shadow fluff brush
- Neutral eye shadow (similar to your natural skin color)
- Black kohl eyeliner pencil
- Smudge brush
- Black eye shadow
- Crease brush
- Cotton swab
- Eye-makeup remover
- White eyeliner pencil (with a blunted tip)
- Concealer brush
- Concealer

TIME IT TAKES
15 minutes

HOW TO DO IT

❶ With the eye shadow fluff brush, apply the neutral eye shadow to the eyelid from the lash line all the way up to the eyebrow.

❷ With the black kohl eyeliner pencil, apply the black liner to the outer rim of your top eyelid. Start at the outer corner of your eye, following your natural lash line in toward the inner corner of your eye.

❸ With the same eyeliner pencil, shade in your eyelid from the lash line and then slightly up past the crease (but not all the way to the eyebrow).

❹ With the same eyeliner pencil, line your bottom eyelid with a thick line. When approaching the outer corners of your eye, pull the line out past your natural eye line to give your eye an almond shape.

❺ Dab a bit of black eye shadow onto the smudge brush and tap the brush to release any excess. Then, apply the shadow over all of the eyeliner on your top lid, which will soften the look a bit. This also sets the liner to make sure it does not wear off.

❻ With the crease brush, blend the black shadow above the crease by moving the brush back and forth (like a windshield wiper) in the crease.

❼ With the same crease brush, pull the eye shadow out just barely past your eyelid to the imaginary angled line that connects the outside corner of your eye and the outside edge of your eyebrow.

❽ Clean any wayward shadow that may have fallen onto your cheeks using a cotton swab and eye-makeup remover.

❾ With the concealer brush, apply concealer in light tapping motions to the darker skin under the eye (typically where bags form). If this takes off some of your liner under the eye, you may need to reapply.

❿ With the smudge brush, smudge the under-the-eye eyeliner line to thicken and blur the line.

⓫ With the white eyeliner, line the inner rims (waterline) of your entire upper and lower lids.

ELIZABETH TAYLOR (1932 –)

Elizabeth (Liz) Taylor got her first break in acting when she was just 10 years old, starring in *There's One Born Every Minute* (1942). Luckily, the film's title didn't apply to Elizabeth, who managed to successfully transition from kid star to adult A-lister—no easy feat in fickle Hollywood. Over the past seven decades, she's established herself as a standout performer and won two Academy Awards. She has also been known for her juicy private life, famously marrying eight times (twice to costar Richard Burton), and collecting world-famous jewels and countless mentions in various gossip columns along the way.

But Elizabeth also made a name for herself in the beauty world when she appeared as the title role in the 1963 hit film *Cleopatra*. In the movie, in which she played an Egyptian Pharaoh, she wore a look that came to be known as the Cleopatra eye. The main components of the look—a drawn-out lash line, bright eye shadow, and dark black eyeliner—are believed to have been makeup staples back in the real Cleopatra's time, in ancient Rome. With the help of her raven hair, strong brows, and violet eyes, Elizabeth revived this exotic style and offered women all over the world a new take on a bold, ancient look.

Essential Elizabeth

- *National Velvet* (film, 1944)
- *Cat on a Hot Tin Roof* (film, 1958)
- *Butterfield 8* (film, 1960)
- *Cleopatra* (film, 1963)
- *Elizabeth Taylor: My Love Affair with Jewelry* (autobiography, 2002)

"*When I was younger, for a long time I didn't wear any makeup in films; when I did start to wear makeup, I always did it myself.***"**

—Elizabeth Taylor

CLEOPATRA EYES

WORKS BEST ON

Anyone

TOOLS NEEDED

- Eye shadow fluff brush
- Neutral base eye shadow (similar to your natural skin color)
- Teal blue eye shadow
- Crease brush
- Angled brow brush
- Light brown eye shadow (in the same shade or slightly lighter than your brow)
- Black eyeliner pencil (sharpened, with the tip lightly tapped a few times to slightly dull the point)
- Black mascara

TIME IT TAKES

10 minutes

HOW TO DO IT

❶ With the eye shadow fluff brush, apply the neutral eye shadow to your eyelid from your lash line all the way up to your eyebrow.

❷ With the same fluff brush, apply the teal blue shadow to your eyelid from your lash line to the crease.

❸ Use the crease brush to blend the teal blue shadow with the neutral base shadow at the crease, so you do not have a harsh line between the two.

❹ With the angled brow brush, apply the light brown shadow to your eyebrow, filling in your brow, where the hair naturally grows, in short, vertical motions.

❺ With the black eye pencil, line the outer rim of your top eyelid. Start in the middle of your lash line and draw a medium thick line down toward the outside corner of your eye. Then go back to the middle point where you started and draw a medium thick line down toward the inside corner of your eye. (The line will be more precise if you draw the line in these two steps, rather than just drawing one long line.) Repeat step for the outer rim of your bottom eyelid.

Also Seen On

Siouxsie Sioux

Zandra Rhodes

Christina Aguilera

❻ With the black eyeliner pencil, lightly mark the point out past your natural lash line where you want the drawn-out eyeliner line to end. From there, holding your pencil so that the tip points directly toward the face at a 90-degree angle, draw the line inward to meet the top line you've already drawn.

❼ With the fluff brush, pull the teal eye shadow out along the drawn-out pencil line you just created.

❽ Apply a heavy coat of black mascara to your top and bottom lashes.

PRO TIP

To create a softer version of the look, skip steps 2–4 and 7, using only the neutral base shadow, black eye pencil and mascara. To create a more dramatic look, like Elizabeth has in the photo, pull the blue shadow all the way up to the brow.

MADONNA (1958 –)

Pop music powerhouse Madonna has released 14 albums (nine of which have gone platinum) and won seven Grammys in her decades-spanning career; she also acted in several films (winning a Golden Globe nomination for the title role in *Evita*), and authored several books. And throughout it all, she's constantly altered her public persona. Marilyn Monroe copycat, naughty S&M dominatrix, geisha girl, urban cowgirl, neo-disco diva, and Goth chick—Madonna has paid homage to all.

But it was her original look as a ragtag temptress that is best remembered, and that earned her a reputation for fearless bravado. When she first came onto the scene in 1982 with her chart-topping single "Everybody," she donned lacey thrift store treasures, ratty hair, and heavy makeup that consisted of thick coats of mascara and eyeliner, a faux beauty mark (see page 67), and colorful, brow-reaching eye shadow. Sometimes, she'd paint her lids in a sunset of oranges, sometimes in wild pinks, sometimes mauves, greys, and blacks, but always with the more-is-more style that defined Madonna and, eventually, the entire '80s decade.

> **"***I am my own experiment. I am my own work of art.***"**
> —Madonna

Overnight, women worldwide started imitating the Material Girl's gritty, DIY look and her most alluring trait: the unabashed confidence that she brought to the stage, TV, and big screen. Madonna wasn't particularly tall, skinny, or classically beautiful, but she inspired generations with her message that all you need to create your own style is a vision and some guts to go with it.

Essential Madonna

- "Like a Virgin"
  (music video, 1984)

- *Desperately Seeking Susan*
  (film, 1985)

- *Who's That Girl?* (film, 1987)

- "Like a Prayer"
  (music video, 1989)

- *Evita* (film, 1996)

MULTI-COLORED EYE SHADOW

WORKS BEST ON
Anyone

TOOLS NEEDED

- Eye shadow fluff brush
- Three different shades of eye shadow (any colors: one light, one medium, one dark)
- Two crease brushes

TIME IT TAKES
5 minutes

HOW TO DO IT

❶ With the eye shadow fluff brush, apply the lightest color shadow to your eyelid from your lash line all the way up to your eyebrow.

❷ With the same fluff brush, apply the medium color on top of the light color, but only from your lash line to the crease.

Also Seen On

Cyndi Lauper
Joan Collins
M.I.A.

❸ With one crease brush, apply the darkest color, only on the actual crease line, from the outer corner to the middle of the crease.

❹ With the other crease brush, blend colors and remove any hard lines along the crease of your eye.

PRO TIP

To select eye shadow colors for this look, consider the following two options. For a look that is monochromatic, try varying shades of the same color, like lilac as the base color, medium purple on the eyelid, and dark purple in the crease; for a dichromatic look, try two shades of one color and one contrasting color, like lilac as the base color, medium purple on the eyelid, and dark green on the crease. Monochromatic is a more natural look that is best for everyday wear, while dichromatic is more dramatic and best for a night out.

RAQUEL WELCH (1940 –)

EYES

Most people identify Raquel Welch with her breakout camp classic film, *One Million Years B.C.* (1966). In the movie, she fights cavemen and prehistoric beasts in nothing more than a torn deerskin bikini, mukluk boots, and layers of fake eyelashes. After the movie's release, a pinup image of Raquel in all of her cavegirl glory quickly became the best-selling poster of its time.

Raquel retained her reputation as a sex symbol for many years, playing other dishy roles like a Viennese prostitute in *The Oldest Profession* (1967) and a woman representing the deadly sin, Lust, in *Bedazzled* (1967). But she also went on to do more serious acting in made-for-television dramatic movies like *Right to Die* (1987) and *Scandal in a Small Town* (1988). Through it all, she held onto one part of her B.C. costume as a part of her regular beauty routine: her false lashes. Welch has even publicly declared that she never leaves home without them. So when she was asked to design her own limited-edition makeup collection for MAC in 2007, it's no surprise that her first order of business was to create a line of signature faux lashes.

Also Seen On

Kim Kardashian
Jennifer Lopez
Eva Mendes

> " *[At the beginning of my career] I became 'Raquel Welch bigger-than-life sex symbol'. Everything real about me was swept aside.* "
>
> —Raquel Welch

Essential Raquel

- *One Million Years B.C.* (film, 1966)

- *Bedazzled* (film, 1967)

- *The Three Musketeers: The Queen's Diamonds* (film, 1973)

- *Raquel: Beyond the Cleavage* (autobiography, 2010)

FAUX LASHES

WORKS BEST ON
Anyone

TOOLS NEEDED
- Eyelash curler
- Mascara (in a color that most closely matches your natural eyelashes)
- False lashes (one set of two strips)
- Scissors
- Black lash adhesive
- Tweezers

TIME IT TAKES
15 minutes

HOW TO DO IT

❶ With the eyelash curler, curl your real lashes. Place the lash curler as close to your lash line as possible and curl each set of lashes for at least 10 seconds.

❷ Apply 1–2 light coats of mascara to your top and bottom lashes. Hold the mascara wand vertically and brush the wand side to side and back and forth across your lashes with the tip of the wand to apply mascara as close to your lash line as possible. This method will help separate lashes and coat the lashes on the inside corner of your eye.

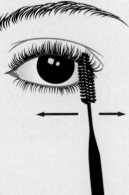

❸ Pick an eye (right or left) to start with. Take the strip of lashes that correspond to that eye and hold it with two hands between your thumb and pointer fingers. (You can tell which strip corresponds with which eye because the longest lashes on the strip are designed to match

up with the outer lashes of your eye.) If the strip of lashes is too straight, move it in a wave pattern to loosen it and help bend it into a curl.

❹ Measure the strip of lashes to your eye by holding it up to your lash line. If it is too long, cut it to fit. Cut from the outside of the lash (the longer hairs) rather than from the inside of the lash (the shorter hairs).

❺ Place a touch of lash adhesive along the entire lash line of the false lashes. Let the glue sit for a second or blow on it to dry it a bit (but not completely).

❻ Grab the center of the adhesive strip of the lashes with the tweezers and place the adhesive-covered strip to the center of your eyelid just above your lash line, lining up the fake lashes with your real ones. (Don't let the lashes get too close to the inner edge of your eye as they will become quickly irritating.) Then, affix the rest of the strip to your lash line by tapping the adhesive strip into place with the tweezers, working your way out to one edge and then the other. The lashes may feel a little heavy at first, but your eyes will adjust. Repeat these steps for the other eye.

❼ Apply another coat of mascara to the false lashes if needed.

> ### PRO TIP
> To keep from blinking while applying false lashes, tilt your head back while continuing to look straight into the mirror.

SOPHIA LOREN (1934 –)

EYES

Sophia Loren has appeared in nearly 100 films since 1950 and won 49 awards for her work, including four Golden Globes and an Academy Award for Best Actress in *Two Women* (1960). And if there were awards given for contributions to the beauty world, Sophia would have no doubt garnered one for meticulous makeup application.

Throughout her career, Sophia has often been known to do her own makeup for movies and public appearances, and she has done it in such a painstakingly perfect way that she's often rendered on-set makeup artists useless. She is, in particular, a pro at executing perfectly applied eye makeup. In the '60s, Loren shaved off her once thick brows and repainted them on with miniscule individual strokes to create two perfect lines—a look that was hard to achieve with actual hairs. She also proved herself a master at painting on a flicked, cat eye (see page 50) with notoriously difficult-to-use liquid liner, exaggerating her exotic eyes and inspiring women to do the same. But the most impressive trick in her beauty repertoire is her detailed mascara application, in which she applies mascara one microthin lash at a time. While most women don't have the time for this painstaking amount of precision, modern techniques have been developed to help women mimic this process and get the same stunning effect.

Essential Sophia

- *Two Women* (film, 1960)
- *Man of La Mancha* (film, 1972)
- *Sophia Loren: Her Own Story* (film, 1980)
- *Sophia Loren's Recipes and Memories* (memoir and cookbook, 1998)
- *Sophia Style* (style guide, 2001)
- *Nine* (film, 2009)

PERFECTLY PRECISE MASCARA

WORKS BEST ON
Anyone

TOOLS NEEDED
- Eyelash curler
- Eyelash primer
- Black mascara
- Dry toothbrush

TIME IT TAKES
3 minutes

HOW TO DO IT

❶ With the eyelash curler, curl your upper lashes. Place the lash curler as close to your lash line as possible and curl each set of lashes for 60 seconds.

❷ Apply the eyelash primer to your upper and lower lashes. (This will make your lashes look fuller.)

❸ Apply two light coats of mascara to the top and bottom lashes. Hold the mascara wand vertically and brush the wand side to side and back and forth across your lashes with the tip of the wand to apply mascara as close to the lash line as possible. This method will help separate lashes and coat the lashes on the inside corner of your eye.

❹ With the dry toothbrush, brush your top lashes from the underside, from the lash line to the tips. This will remove excess mascara and further separate the lashes. If your bottom lashes are clumpy, then brush those, too—this time brushing from the top side.

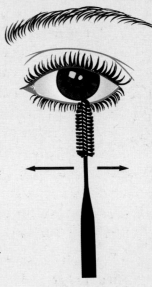

Also Seen On

Zooey Deschanel
Reese Witherspoon
Selena Gomez

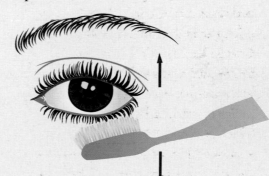

❝ *Nothing makes a woman more beautiful than the belief that she is beautiful.* ❞
—Sophia Loren

PRO TIP

To get more out of your eyelash curler, heat it up. To do this, blow hot air from your hair dryer onto your eyelash curler for three to five seconds. Immediately after, curl your lashes on one eye, being careful not to touch the curler to your skin. Next, apply mascara as directed above. Then repeat with your other eye.

TWIGGY (1949 –)

EYES

In the mid-1960s, amid the swinging London Youthquake scene of miniskirts, go-go boots, and innovative youth culture, a 16-year-old schoolgirl named Leslie Hornby became an overnight sensation. Quickly nicknamed Twiggy because of her skinny frame, this super tiny supermodel—who wore a short pixie cut, white-out lips (see page 16), and otherworldly Kewpie doll eyelashes—was soon pegged "The Face of '66" by London's *Express* newspaper.

While Twiggy's entire look was fresh and unique, it was her lashes that really made a statement. Lashes of previous decades were long, thin, and slightly darkened, but Twiggy's were plumped up to cartoonish proportions. The look was initially the idea of Twiggy's manager and mentor Justin de Villeneuve, who was inspired by the eyelashes on a doll that belonged to his sister. But it wasn't an easy look to achieve; Twiggy would later admit that her make-up—which included pancake foundation, pale lips, and her signature lashes—would take a painstaking 90 minutes to apply.

Twiggy and her drawn-on lashes started to create a Twiggy mania. *Life* and *Newsweek* ran major stories on the craze, and *The New Yorker* featured Twiggy on nearly 100 pages in 1967 alone. But perhaps the biggest testament to Twiggy's permeation into pop culture was the birth of a "Twiggy" Barbie that same year. Now there was a doll that sported a look that had originated from a doll itself.

Essential Twiggy

- *The Boy Friend* (film, 1971)

- *Twiggy's Guide to Looking Good* (autobiographical style guide, 1986)

- *Twiggy in Black and White* (autobiography, 1998)

"*Whether you're thin, fat, small, dark, blond, redhead—you wanna be something else.*"

—Twiggy

KEWPIE DOLL LASHES

WORKS BEST ON
Longer lashes

TOOLS NEEDED
- Fine pointed liner brush
- Black liquid or gel liner
- Eyelash primer
- Black mascara
- Strip of false, clumped-together lashes and lash adhesive (optional)

TIME IT TAKES
15 minutes

HOW TO DO IT

❶ With the liner brush, draw false lashes on your skin underneath your eye using the black liquid or gel liner (the false lashes should originate from your actual lash line). Start by creating longer lashes on the outside of your eye and continue making progressively shorter lashes as you move inward.

❷ With the eyelash curler, curl your top lashes. Place the lash curler as close to your lash line as possible and curl each set of lashes for 30 seconds.

❸ Brush the eyelash primer onto your top and bottom lashes the same way you would brush on mascara. (This lengthens your lashes and helps you clump them together.)

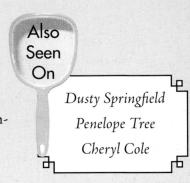

Also Seen On

Dusty Springfield
Penelope Tree
Cheryl Cole

❹ While the primer is still wet, apply 1–2 coats of masara to both the top and bottom lashes.

❺ Use the tip of the mascara brush to clump your top lashes into groups. If your lashes are not long and thick enough to achieve this effect, try using false lashes on the top lids. (See page 39 for instructions on how to apply false lashes.)

JOAN JETT (1958 –)

In 1975, when Joan Jett was 17 years old, she joined The Runaways, a pioneering all-girl rock group that was part of the Los Angeles rock scene. Jett sported a glam-meets-gritty look, wearing lots of gloss and glittery makeup along with leather jackets and jeans when performing around town. In the years to come, the guitarist and singer paved the way for women in rock to wail with the best of the boys, all while starting a new beauty trend with her rocker-chic style.

Joan can't be totally credited for originating the key components of her style—she borrowed her signature shag haircut from rock legend David Bowie, and her dark, smoky eye makeup from past beauty icons like screen legends Ava Gardner and Katharine Hepburn. But it was how she repackaged these elements—incorporating things like denim and bandana-wrapped wrists—and presented them with her aggressive stage presence that made the recycled

look new. Her take on the smoky eye was especially fresh. What was once thought to be a style reserved for smoldering screen goddesses of the 1930s was now the look of the edgy, bad girl.

Essential Joan

- *I Love Rock N Roll* (album, 1981)
- *Joan Jett and the Blackhearts: Live!* (DVD, 2001)
- *The Runaways* (biopic, 2010)
- *Joan Jett* (photographic biography, 2010)

> *Girls have got balls. They're just a little higher up, that's all.*
>
> —Joan Jett

SMOKY EYES

WORKS BEST ON
Anyone

TOOLS NEEDED
- Eye shadow fluff brush
- Neutral base eye shadow (similar to your skin color)
- Black eyeliner pencil
- Smudge brush
- Black eye shadow
- Concealer brush
- Concealer
- Black mascara

TIME IT TAKES
10 minutes

HOW TO DO IT

❶ With the eye shadow fluff brush, apply the neutral eye shadow to your eyelid from your lash line all the way up to your eyebrow.

❷ With the black eyeliner pencil, apply the black liner to the outer rim of your top eyelid. Start at the outer corner of your eye, following your natural lash line in toward the inner corner of your eye. Repeat this step for your bottom lash line. This line doesn't have to be precise since you are going to go over it with the eye shadow. (Using the pencil first ensures that you get a very dark outline.)

❸ With the smudge brush, apply black eye shadow by drawing over the top and bottom eyeliner lines you just applied. The top and bottom lines should look soft and smudged. Reapply shadow until you get the desired intensity.

❹ With the concealer brush, apply concealer in light tapping motions to the darker skin under your eye (typically where bags form) and to the space between the inner corner of your eye and your nose.

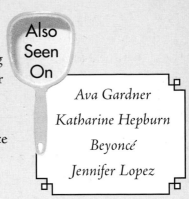

Also Seen On

Ava Gardner
Katharine Hepburn
Beyoncé
Jennifer Lopez

❺ With the tip of your pointer or pinky finger, gently tap the concealer to blend it in, so there are no lines where the concealer ends.

❻ Apply two light coats of mascara to the top and bottom lashes. Hold the mascara wand vertically and brush the wand side to side and back and forth across your lashes with the tip of the wand to apply mascara as close to the lash line as possible. This method will help separate lashes and coat the lashes on the inside corner of your eye.

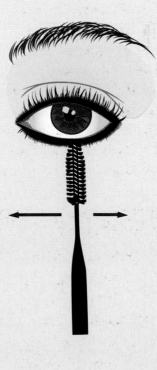

GRACE JONES (1948 –)

Masculine or feminine? Singer or actress? Model or Muse? When it comes to Grace Jones, the answer is all of the above. The Jamaican-born, New York-raised beauty made her mark in the annals of pop culture by producing nearly a dozen pop-rock albums, starring in films such as *Boomerang* (1992), and walking the runway for everyone from fashion designer Issey Miyake to the clothing company Diesel. But whether it was on stage, screen, or catwalk, Grace has always aimed to shock the world with her sparkly femme makeup, masculine, blunt flat-top hair, and overall androgynous style.

Like many trendsetting stars, the looks that Grace sported while in the public eye were often too extreme for the average woman to imitate. When playing villain-ess May Day in the James Bond flick *A View to A Kill* (1985), Grace was made up in dramatic, hyper-red rouge. On her *Island Life* (1985) album cover, she posed nearly nude, with her sculpted body glistening in a glossy sheen. But early on, Grace did have one look that attracted

followers: metallic eye shadow. She wore it on her 1970s album covers and the look influenced the disco divas of the decade, while serving as a fashion forecast for the neon and geometric shapes that dominated '80s style. Today, metallic shadow can still be seen by models wearing extreme looks on the runways, and on girls who want a little extra shimmer when out on the dance floor.

> **"***In the seventies and eighties we all had our fun, and now and then we went really too far. But ultimately, it required a certain amount of clear thinking, a lot of hard work, and good makeup to be accepted as a freak.***"**
>
> —Grace Jones

Essential Grace

- *Grace Jones—Live in NYC* **(recorded concert, 1981)**
- *A View to a Kill* **(film, 1985)**
- *Boomerang* **(film, 1992)**
- *20th Century Masters: Millennium Collection* **(album, 2003)**

METALLIC EYE SHADOW

WORKS BEST ON

Anyone

TOOLS NEEDED

- Eye shadow fluff brush
- Matte neutral eye shadow (similar to your skin color)
- 2 crease brushes
- Angled eyeliner brush
- Metallic eye shadow (any color with shimmer, not glitter)
- Black eye shadow
- Black mascara

TIME IT TAKES

5 minutes

HOW TO DO IT

❶ With the eye shadow fluff brush, apply the matte neutral eye shadow to your eyelid from your lash line all the way up to your eyebrow.

❷ With one crease brush, apply the metallic eye shadow to the outer corner of your eye, creating a right-angled triangle that sits between your lash line and the crease.

❸ With the other crease brush, blend the neutral eye shadow and metallic shadow, blurring the outlines of the triangle.

PRO TIP

To make this look more dramatic, line the outer rim of your bottom eyelid with black shadow.

❹ Dab a bit of black eye shadow onto the angled eyeliner brush and tap the brush to release any excess. With the angled eyeliner brush, line your upper lash line with a very light layer of black eye shadow. Start at the outside of your eye and move inward toward your nose, holding the brush steady so that the edge of the shadow stays sharp and defined.

Also Seen On

Rihanna

Alicia Keys

Katy Perry

❺ With the first crease brush (the same one used to apply the metallic shadow), apply a thin veil of black shadow over the entire metallic triangle to tone down the metallic shadow. (The metallic shadow should still show through.)

❻ Apply two light coats of mascara to the top and bottom lashes. Hold the mascara wand vertically and brush the wand side to side and back and forth across your lashes with the tip of the wand to apply mascara as close to the lash line as possible. This method will help separate lashes and coat the lashes on the inside corner of your eye. (See page 39 for illustration.)

AISHWARYA RAI BACHCHAN (1973 –)

In 1994, in an effort to bring her country to the world stage, a barely known 21-year-old Indian model named Aishwarya Rai entered the Miss World pageant—and won. After that, movie offers from Bollywood (India's booming film industry) instantly poured in, putting the young beauty on her way to worldwide stardom. Aishwarya has since appeared in nearly 50 films, and has become one of India's highest-paid actresses. In 2003, she married fellow actor Abhishek Bachchan, and became half of India's most popular Bollywood couple. The following year, she made her American film debut in *Bride and Prejudice* (2004). But while she's gained great fame in the world of film, it's her stunning beauty and striking grey-green eyes that have kept the international public in absolute adoration.

To bring attention to her eyes (which are so famous that one fan created an entire website dedicated to them), Aishwarya often lines them with a microthin stroke of dark, smoldering eyeliner. The look, which has become her red-carpet staple, is mysterious and sexy. But it's also classy and clean, which makes it an appropriate style for the star who famously upholds her traditional Indian values (she refuses to kiss co-stars onscreen out of loyalty to her husband). Despite all of the hoopla around Aishwarya's peepers, she knows that, in the end, eyes are best used for seeing with. As a testament to this, she's publically announced that hers will be donated to medicine when she dies.

Essential Aishwarya

- *Devdas* (film, 2002)
- *Bride & Prejudice* (film, 2004)
- *The Mistress of Spices* (film, 2005)

> *Life will take its toll on all of us. We get injured, we get old. It's really sad to try to run away from these harsh realities of life. Looks are not everything. I am not going to look beautiful all the time.*
> —Aishwarya Rai Bachchan

SMOLDERING, MICROTHIN EYELINER

WORKS BEST ON
Anyone

TOOLS NEEDED
- Black eyeliner pencil (with a blunted tip)
- Cotton swab
- Black mascara

TIME IT TAKES
5 minutes

HOW TO DO IT

❶ With the black eyeliner, line the inner rims (waterline) of your entire upper and lower lids.

❷ Line your lash line (the place where the lash grows out of the lid) of both your upper and lower lids. Repeat steps 1 and 2 until you get the desired intensity.

❸ With the cotton swab, gently remove any stray liner that falls outside of your lash line on both your upper and lower lids.

❹ Apply 1–2 light coats of mascara to your top and bottom lashes. Hold the mascara wand vertically and brush the wand side to side and back and forth across your lashes with the tip of the wand to apply mascara as close to the lash line as possible. This method will help separate lashes and coat the lashes on the inside corner of your eye.

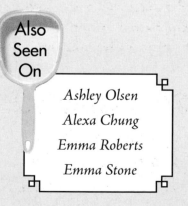

Also Seen On

Ashley Olsen

Alexa Chung

Emma Roberts

Emma Stone

ANGELINA JOLIE (1975 –)

A woman-of-the-world who leads a luxurious yet nomadic life with dashing, movie-star beau Brad Pitt and their band of international children, Angelina Jolie is known for her adventurous nature—both on and off the big screen. In her films, she portrays kick-ass women in action flicks like *Lara Croft: Tomb Raider* (2001), *Mr. and Mrs. Smith* (2005), and *Salt* (2010). When she's not acting, the star is known for riding motorcycles, piloting planes, and assisting people in war-torn countries. So it's no surprise that Angelina has made cat eye makeup a staple of her red-carpet style; it's a look that embodies the feline qualities of curiosity, playfulness, and adventurousness.

Of course, Angelina did not invent this look. A long line of beauties who came before her also wore it well: Barbara Eden in *I Dream of Jeannie* (1965–70), Brigitte Bardot in *Contempt* (1963), and Anne Bancroft in *The Graduate* (1967) to name a few. But Angelina's cat eye is different not only because she draws a thinner, more understated line, but because she brings her own daredevil, post-feminist, and utterly modern feel to the look.

Essential Angelina

- *Girl, Interrupted* (film, 1999)
- *Lara Croft: Tomb Raider* (film, 2001)
- *Notes From My Travels* (autobiographical travelogue, 2003)
- *Mr. & Mrs. Smith* (film, 2005)
- *Salt* (film, 2010)

"*If you ask people what they've always wanted to do, most people haven't done it. That breaks my heart.***"**

—Angelina Jolie

CAT EYES

WORKS BEST ON
Anyone

TOOLS NEEDED
• Black liquid eyeliner (with applicator)

TIME IT TAKES
10 minutes

HOW TO DO IT

❶ Tilt your head back a bit so that when you are looking in the mirror, it feels like you are looking down on your reflection. (This way, you can see what you are doing while applying the liner without having to blink. This also keeps your eyelid smooth; a closed eye becomes too wrinkled to apply liner.)

Also Seen On

Sophia Loren

Brigitte Bardot

Zandra Rhodes

Leighton Meester

❷ With the liquid liner (using its built-in applicator), apply a medium to thick line along half of the outer rim of your upper lash line. To do this, start in the center of your eyelid and move out to the outside corner of your eye. (If there's too much liner on the applicator, wipe a bit off onto the back of your hand.) Just before you reach the corner, pull the line out a little past the corner of your eye, and slightly upward. (You can carry this line as far as you like, though a quarter of an inch is the most common.) This will open up your eye instead of making it droop.

❸ With the liquid liner, connect the end point of the line you've just drawn to the outer corner of your bottom lash line, creating a triangular shape.

❹ Fill in the triangular shape.

❺ Take the liquid liner applicator tip to the center of your upper eyelid where you started your line in Step 2, and complete the line, drawing out to the inside corner of your eye.

❻ With the liquid liner, line the outer rim of your bottom lash line. To do this, start in the center of your lash line and move out to the outside corner of your eye. Then, place the liquid liner applicator where you started the line and complete the thin line, drawing out to the inside corner of your eye.

PRO TIP
Liquid liner dries and stains pretty quickly. To erase any mistakes when lining, keep cotton swabs and eye-makeup remover handy.

PRO TIP
To get the same look with a more user-friendly medium, try using a freshly sharpened eyeliner pencil instead of liquid liner. When lining your eye, make small dots (close enough to touch one another) along your upper lash line. When you reach the end of your natural lash line, slant the eyeliner line upward at a 45-degree angle and draw out about a quarter of an inch.

CHER (1946 –)

Singer and actor Cher first took the stage at age 18, when she and her 29-year-old husband Sonny Bono debuted as the musical duo, Sonny and Cher. In the nine years they performed together, from 1965 to 1974, the two recorded a string of number one hits—most famously, the classic "I Got You, Babe"—and cracked jokes on their hit variety show, *The Sonny and Cher Comedy Hour*. Each week, viewers tuned in to see Cher in a new attention-grabbing outfit, many created by the famous costume designer and longtime Cher collaborator Bob Mackie. Designs included fur vests, glittering headdresses and body-skimming gowns dripping in sequins. Cher had become more than an entertainer—she'd become a flashy fashion plate.

Cher later found success as a solo musical artist and serious actress (she won an Academy Award for her role in *Moonstruck* in 1987), but even as she moved from camp to high-brow, she never gave up her love for glam and glitz. Her outfits have continued to be nothing short of outrageous, and her makeup has reflected her fashion sense. Sparkles, bright blue eye shadow, and high-gloss eyelids have become synonymous with Cher style. And the look has become so popular that makeup companies now produce color-spiked eye glosses for those who want to achieve it on the go.

Essential Cher

- *Gypsys, Tramps and Thieves* (album, 1971)
- *The Witches of Eastwick* (film, 1987)
- *Moonstruck* (film, 1987)
- *The First Time* (memoir, 1999)
- *Burlesque* (film, 2010)

"*I only use a mirror to see if my makeup is on right.*"
—Cher

GLOSSY EYELIDS

WORKS BEST ON
Anyone

TOOLS NEEDED
- Eye shadow fluff brush
- Eye shadow (any shade)
- Eyeliner pencil in a similar shade to the shadow (black with grey shadow, cobalt, or navy eyeliner with blue shadow)
- Concealer brush
- Clear, thin unscented lip balm (in a pot, not a stick)

TIME IT TAKES
10 minutes

HOW TO DO IT

❶ With the eye shadow fluff brush, apply the eye shadow to your eyelid, from your lash line to the crease.

❷ With the eyeliner pencil, line the outer rim of your top eyelid. Start in the middle of your lash line and draw a medium thick line down toward the outside corner of your eye. Then go back to the middle point where you started and draw a medium thick line down toward the inside corner of your eye. (The line will be more precise if you draw it in these two steps, rather than just drawing one long line.)

❸ Apply two light coats of mascara to the top and bottom lashes. Hold the mascara wand vertically and brush the wand side to side and back and forth across your lashes with the tip of the wand to apply mascara as close to the lash line as possible. This method will help separate lashes and coat the lashes on the inside corner of your eye. If desired, apply false lashes. (See page 39.)

❹ With the concealer brush, apply clear lip balm to your eyelid, from your lash line all the way up to your eyebrow.

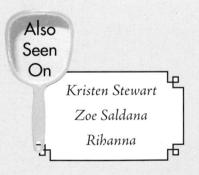

Also Seen On

Kristen Stewart

Zoe Saldana

Rihanna

(See page 39.)

PRO TIP

This look is best for taking photos or doing something with little activity. It tends to get messed up easily, so it's not really practical for a night out on the town.

BROWS

When we want to know if someone is surprised, worried, confused, or angry, we look to the face's ultimate expressers— the eyebrows. These strips of hair not only separate our eye area from our foreheads, they also reveal what a person is feeling without a word. So it makes sense that we spend so much time grooming them. But eyebrow grooming is not new. The ancient Egyptians, Romans, Greeks, and Victorian-period English all did drastic things to their brows. In more modern history, icons have worn everything from bushy brows (Brooke Shields, page 62) to delicate brows (Kate Moss, page 60), and have even been as bold to remove their brows altogether (Sophia Loren, page 40) and draw them back on as they like! While modern-day brow trends quickly move from slight to strong and back again, one thing is certain: plucking and penciling are here to stay.

KATE MOSS (1974 –)

A teenage model with delicate features, limp hair, and a "petite" frame (5' 7" is considered short by modeling standards), Kate Moss shot to fame in the early 1990s after being given her big break by designer Calvin Klein. Soon, she was seen everywhere—on magazine pages, giant billboards over Times Square, and television—representing one of the biggest names in fashion.

Whether she was modeling jeans in a TV spot or wearing nothing at all for the brand's Obsession fragrance ads, Kate was always seen with soft, delicate brows. This look, combined with her waifish figure, put her in step with the heroin-chic trend that was dominating the grunge rock scene of the '90s, and with the minimalist vibe that went on to characterize the decade. Girls everywhere started waxing and plucking their brows to next-to-nothing strips. (Some did this a bit too often, and learned the hard way that brows don't always grow back after overplucking.) Kate went on to become known for her innovative high/low fashion, her self-designed clothing and handbag collections for Topshop

and Longchamp, and her party-heavy lifestyle. But she'll always be remembered for the delicacy of both her figure and her ultra-plucked eyebrows.

Essential Kate

- •*Kate: The Kate Moss Book* (photographic autobiography, **1997**)
- •"I Just Don't Know What to Do With Myself" (White Stripes music video, **2003**)
- •*Kate Moss: Style* (style book, **2008**)
- •*Kate Moss* (photo book, **2010**)

> "*People think your success is just a matter of having a pretty face. But it's easy to be chewed up and spat out. You've got to stay ahead of the game to be able to stay in it.*"
>
> —Kate Moss

DELICATELY SHAPED BROWS

WORKS BEST ON
Faces with delicate features

TOOLS NEEDED
- Powder brush
- Powder (loose or pressed)
- Light brown eyeliner pencil
- Tweezers

TIME IT TAKES
8 minutes

HOW TO DO IT

❶ Dab a bit of powder onto the powder brush and tap the brush to release any excess. Sweep brush across your eyebrow and the surrounding skin. This will prevent the hairs from sticking to the skin so that you can pluck them easily.

❷ With the light brown eyeliner pencil, draw a line along the length of the bottom edge of your brow.

❸ With the tweezers, remove all the hairs that fall on the penciled line, as well as any stray hairs that fall below it. Pluck in the same direction that the hair grows to help remove the hair by the root instead of breaking the hair off where it meets the skin.

❹ Pluck any wayward hairs above the brow line that clearly don't join the rest of your brow (but do this sparingly, leaving the natural shape of the upper edge of the brow line intact).

❺ If you feel that your brow is still too full, repeat Step 2 by drawing a line that follows the line of the very bottom edge of your newly plucked brow, and then repeat Step 3. But be careful not to overpluck, and to stay with the natural shape of your eyebrow.

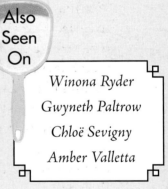

Also Seen On

Winona Ryder
Gwyneth Paltrow
Chloë Sevigny
Amber Valletta

PRO TIP

To prevent overplucking, go slowly and be conservative as you pluck. It's harder to fix overplucked brows than underplucked brows, and brow hair doesn't always grow back if plucked too much. If you are unsure of how much to pluck, have your brows shaped by a professional and then simply maintain the look by cleaning up the brow line at home. Use tweezers instead of wax, since they allow you to be more precise.

MARLENE DIETRICH (1901 – 1992)

After achieving success as a film actor in her native Germany, Marlene Dietrich came to the US in 1930 to work with Paramount Pictures. She quickly became a Hollywood superstar, making seven films with acclaimed director Josef von Sternberg in the 1930s alone. She was the first German-born actress to be nominated for an Oscar and was honored with the US War Department's Medal of Freedom in 1947 for refusing to work for the Nazi film industry and for entertaining US troops. But Marlene was also a beauty innovator; while most stars of the time were content to have someone else do their makeup, Marlene did her own, inventing an arsenal of clever techniques that later influenced professional makeup artists.

One of Marlene's makeup techniques involved burning a matchstick, dipping it in baby oil, and applying it to her eyelid to create an early version of eye shadow. This move inspired cosmetic heavyweights to create the powdered eye shadows that we wear today. Marlene also painted a white line of makeup down the bridge of her nose to make it look slimmer. This trick is still used today, but with highlighting makeup products. And to make her natural brows more dramatic, Marlene would boldly fill them in with dark, defining pencil. Not all of Marlene's homegrown beauty tricks (like sucking on lemons to tighten her mouth muscles) stood the test of time. But the majority of her innovations have had a significant effect on the world of beauty.

Essential Marlene

- *The Blue Angel* (film, 1930)
- *Morocco* (film, 1930)
- *Shanghai Express* (film, 1932)

> *"The relationship between the makeup man and the film actor is that of accomplices in crime."*
>
> —Marlene Dietrich

DARKENED BROWS

WORKS BEST ON
Anyone

TOOLS NEEDED

- Tweezers
- Brow pencil (a shade lighter than your brows)
- Clear brow fix or tamer
- Spoolie brush or clean disposable mascara wand

TIME IT TAKES
3 minutes

HOW TO DO IT

❶ Pluck your brow as you normally would to fit the shape of your face and eye. Pluck in the same direction that the hair grows to help remove the hair by the root instead of breaking the hair off where it meets the skin. (If you've never done this before, consider having a professional shape your brows at a salon.)

❷ With the brow pencil, start at the inside of your brow (the part closest to your nose) and make a line along the top arch of your brow all the way out to the edge near your temple.

❸ Using small strokes, fill in your brow, where the hair naturally grows, in short, vertical motions. This will create a fuller-looking, more pronounced brow.

❹ Take the spoolie brush or clean disposable mascara wand to brush out your brow and soften the edges of the pencil you just applied. This way the fill-in looks natural. (If you want your brow to have a hard edge, you can skip this step.)

❺ Apply the brow fix or tamer to keep your brows in place.

Also Seen On

Madonna
Camilla Belle
Elizabeth Taylor

When burgeoning Swedish actress Greta Garbo arrived in Hollywood in 1925 to shoot films for MGM, she had already established herself as a leading lady in the Swedish film industry. But to ensure she was screen-ready for her American debut in *Torrent* (1926), she visited Hollywood makeup king Max Factor to help fine-tune her look. Factor immediately went to work sculpting her thick, ungroomed brows. He first plucked them to nothing, and then penciled on thin, high arches to draw attention to her eyes.

The transformation helped Greta become the most popular actress of the '20s and '30s—and eventually one of the highest-paid women in the country. While Greta was certainly lauded for her acting chops (she is said to have invented the Method acting technique), much of her box-office success was due to people's adoration of her timeless beauty and seductive gaze.

Greta's eyebrows—and eyes, in general—created a stir among the public. Before the star came along, women considered eye makeup to be trashy and mainly focused on their lips when using cosmetics. But Greta's tasteful look encouraged even the most wholesome of girls to start penciling on their brows and wearing mascara and eye shadow. Greta, Max Factor, and the Hollywood machine had sparked a new age in American beauty.

> **"**I don't want to be a silly temptress. I cannot see any sense in getting dressed up and doing nothing but tempting men in pictures.**"**
> —Greta Garbo

Essential Greta

- *The Temptress* (film, 1926)
- *Grand Hotel* (film, 1932)
- *Anna Karenina* (film, 1935)
- *Camille* (film, 1936)
- *Conversations with Greta Garbo* (book, 1992)

THIN, ARCHED BROWS

WORKS BEST ON

Large round eyes

TOOLS NEEDED

- Eyebrow pencil to match your brow hair (with a well-sharpened and slightly blunted tip)
- Tweezers
- Eye makeup remover
- Cotton swab
- Clear brow fix or tamer
- Spoolie brush (optional, see Pro Tip)

TIME IT TAKES

20 minutes (less if your brow has already been shaped)

HOW TO DO IT

❶ With the eyebrow pencil, draw a line in a rounded arch, right on the top edge of one brow. The line should be thin and even throughout, tapering off just a little as you near the end of your brow (the part nearest to your ear). Repeat with the other brow. Make sure both eyebrows are even.

❷ With the tweezers, remove all the hairs that do not fall on or close to the penciled line. (Greta plucked all of her brow hair off but that look is too severe for most people; you'll leave a thin line of hair.) Pluck in the same direction that the hair grows to help remove the hair by the root instead of breaking the hair off where it meets the skin.

❸ Remove the eyebrow pencil with a cotton swab and eye makeup remover.

❹ With the eyebrow pencil, draw a new line through the hairs of your newly shaped brows to make the shape look clean and crisp.

❺ Apply the brow fix or tamer to keep your brows in place.

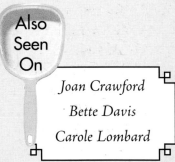

Also Seen On

Joan Crawford
Bette Davis
Carole Lombard

PRO TIP

This is a fun look for every now and then, but don't maintain it for too long. For some, eyebrow hair stops growing back if it's been plucked too many times.

PRO TIP

To keep your brows in line while plucking, use a spoolie brush, combing through the hair occasionally as you pluck. This will give you a clearer picture of what you're working with and when to stop plucking.

BROOKE SHIELDS (1965 –)

BROWS

Brooke Shields started her modeling career at just 11 months old, appearing on television as the Ivory Soap baby. Her big break came at the age of 12 when she played a child prostitue in the controversial film *Pretty Baby* (1978). Audiences were captivated by her young face, pronounced cheekbones and full, unkempt brows, which quickly became known as her most famous attribute.

Her role in *Pretty Baby* led to increased exposure, and soon her image was everywhere. In 1981 alone, she appeared on more than 30 magazine covers and was featured in a very risqué, high-profile Calvin Klein jeans campaign. For this, her most memorable job in her modeling career, designer Calvin Klein personally selected Shields because she possessed a look that was a perfect mixture of masculine and feminine—the unarched, bushy brows, and broad shoulders were manly, while her eyes, cheeks and lips emitted a very delicate and feminine look. Klein's instinct and timing were perfect: After Brooke was seen on television ads, topless and uttering "Nothing gets between me and my Calvins," the company's jeans sales skyrocketed 300 percent. But women worldwide were not only inspired to buy jeans. They also tossed their tweezers and went au naturel with their brows to fully emulate the essence of Brooke.

Essential Brooke

- *Pretty Baby* (film, 1978)
- *The Blue Lagoon* (film, 1980)
- *Endless Love* (film, 1981)
- *On Your Own* (autobiography, 1985)

"*Don't waste a minute not being happy. If one window closes, run to the next window—or break down a door.***"**

—Brooke Shields

NATURAL, FULL BROWS

WORKS BEST ON
Thicker brows

TOOLS NEEDED
- Regular writing pencil
- Brow pencil
- Tweezers
- Eye-makeup remover
- Brow fix or tamer wand

TIME IT TAKES
5 minutes

HOW TO DO IT

❶ Hold the writing pencil vertically in front of your face beside one of the outer edges of your nose. Note where it hits your brow line, and, with the brow pencil, make a mark where the pencil lies. (Mark the side of the pencil closest to the center of your eyes.) This mark will serve as an indicator as to where to stop plucking while removing hairs from in between your eyes. Repeat on the other side of your nose, marking the other eyebrow.

❷ Remove dark hairs that fall in the center of these two marks. Pluck in the same direction that the hair grows to help remove the hair by the root instead of breaking the hair off where it meets the skin.

❸ With the eye-makeup remover, erase the indicator marks you made with the brow pencil.

❹ With the brow fix or tamer wand, brush the brow hairs upward at the section of the brow that is closest to your nose. Then brush the brow outward as you move toward your temple.

Also Seen On

Jennifer Connelly
Ali MacGraw
Lourdes Leon

PRO TIP

To help minimize the pain of plucking, ice the area you plan to pluck for a few minutes before beginning. It also helps to hold the skin taught as you pluck.

SKIN & FACE

Sometimes we look at makeup in the little picture—like when we emphasize the eyes, lips, or brows. But it's also important to see the big picture: the whole face. It starts with a flawless foundation (Iman, page 78) that can help you achieve a perfect-looking complexion. Then, of course, there are the different ways to chisel your cheeks by using blush. And if you want to be creative, you can obtain a masterful overall look like Kate Winslet's no-makeup makeup (page 74) or Uma Thurman's ethereal makeup (page 80). Some women even decorate their faces as if they were pieces of modern art, like Kat Von D and her delicate face tattoos (page 76). Your face really is your base and your playground, and thanks to the groundbreaking innovations of the modern-day cosmetics industry, we have an endless array of products to conceal blemishes, darken and lighten our skin tones, and adorn our beautiful selves to our endless delight.

CINDY CRAWFORD (1966 –)

When Cindy Crawford first entered the modeling world, agents advised her to remove a prominent mole on her face, located just above her upper lip. It was the mid 1980s, a time when American beauty was defined by girl-next-door types like Christie Brinkley (see page 26), and moles were thought to be imperfect and unfashionable. But Cindy refused to remove hers, and wore it like a sexy badge of honor.

Cindy's instincts were right—the people in the fashion industry didn't just tolerate her mole, they fell in love with it. Throughout the '80s and '90s, she became a supermodel reportedly earning up to $20,000 a day for modeling and, along with Madonna, became the most featured cover girl of the time.

Soon, Cindy's popularity brought the beauty mark into the forefront of fashion. Guess clothing designer Georges Marciano began to showcase models with fake beauty marks, and body piercers began giving women the "chrome Crawford" piercing, located just above the upper lip. Cindy's choice to stay true to her natural look changed the status quo. And her name, to this day, remains synonymous with the beauty mark.

SKIN & FACE

66 *Even I don't look like Cindy Crawford in the morning.* **99**

—Cindy Crawford

Essential Cindy

- *Cindy Crawford Shape Your Body Workout* (video, 1992)

- *Fair Game* (film, 1995)

- *Cindy Crawford's Basic Face* (book, 1996)

- *Beautopia* (documentary, 1998)

BEAUTY MARK

WORKS BEST ON
Anyone

TOOLS NEEDED

- Brown/black or black pencil liner or liquid liner
- Fine pointed liner brush
- Powder brush
- Translucent powder (loose or pressed)

TIME IT TAKES
4 minutes

HOW TO DO IT

❶ Choose the placement for the beauty mark. They are usually placed to the side of your upper lip or above your lip, near your nose.

❷ Decide whether to use a pencil liner or liquid liner. If you use a pencil, make sure the tip of the pencil isn't too pointy. If using the liquid, make sure it's waterproof and that there isn't a lot of excess product on the brush when you apply it.

Also Seen On

Madonna

Jean Harlow

Dita Von Teese

Marilyn Monroe

With pencil liner:

❶ Touch the end of the pencil to your face and rotate the pencil between your finger tips.

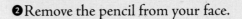

❷ Remove the pencil from your face.

With liquid liner:

❶ Lightly apply the liner as a small dot on your face. (Be careful not to make it too big. The size of a fleck of sea salt should do the trick.) Wait until the liquid is dry and reapply the liner. You can repeat this step until you are satisfied with the darkness of your beauty mark.

❷ When the liner is dry, set it by lightly dusting translucent powder over the beauty mark.

PRO TIP

To balance your beauty mark nicely, use a bright lip color, a trick used by everyone from Dolly Parton (page 88) to Marilyn Monroe (page 22).

PRO TIP

Always put your beauty mark in the same place if you want people to think it's real.

COURTNEY LOVE (1965 –)

Musician Courtney Love emerged on the grunge scene in the early 1990s as the outspoken girlfriend of Nirvana frontman Kurt Cobain. Soon, exposure from the famous relationship helped launch her musical career as the lead singer of rock band Hole. With her self-proclaimed "kinder-whore" look—which consisted of torn babydoll dresses over ripped fishnet stockings and bird's-nest hair adorned with kiddie barrettes—she combined the characteristics of young and sweet with those of tough and reckless. To top off her look, she wore her makeup messy: pink stain on her cheeks, clumpy mascara on her eyes, and smeared lipstick.

But Courtney's haphazard makeup and torn clothing didn't mean she was disinterested in glamour. Despite her rebellion against traditional beauty standards, she still toiled with foundation and rouge with the best of them. It's just that she didn't want to show that she cared. Hers was a look that screamed, "I've got better things to do than freshen up my lipstick."

While Courtney eventually ditched her original look for one that was more refined and put-together, her messy makeup lives on as a favorite style worn by hard-partying club kids. Courtney scoffed at the idea of precision and perfection, and those who follow in her footsteps continue to do the same.

SKIN & FACE

> **"** *I like there to be some testosterone in rock, and it's like I'm the one in the dress who has to provide it.* **"**
>
> —Courtney Love

Essential Courtney

- *Sid and Nancy* (film, 1986)
- *The People vs. Larry Flynt* (film, 1996)
- *Dirty Blonde: The Diaries of Courtney Love* (autobiographical scrapbook, 2006)

MESSY MAKEUP

WORKS BEST ON
Anyone

TOOLS NEEDED
- Black liquid eyeliner
- Black mascara
- Creamy blush
- Red lipstick

TIME IT TAKES
10 minutes

HOW TO DO IT

❶ With the eyeliner, line the top and bottom outer rims of your eyelid, starting from the inside corner of your eye, following your lash line to the outer edge. Let the line be a little messy.

❷ Apply three coats of the mascara to your top lashes and two coats to your bottom lashes (no need to let them dry in between). It will be a bit clumpy—this is part of the look.

❸ With your fingers, apply the creamy blush to the apples of your cheeks in a small tapping, circular motion until you achieve the desired intensity. To find the apples of your cheeks, just smile— the apple is the round area close to your nose. (You can use your fingers to blend the blush so there isn't too hard a line between your blushed and un-blushed skin, but don't blend too well— you want to keep the look messy.)

❹ Apply the red lipstick following your natural lip line. Don't use lip liner here, to keep the look a little messy.

Also Seen On

Tammy Faye Baker
Betsey Johnson
Elizabeth Jagger

PRO TIP

If the look of red, messy lipstick doesn't work for you, try a tinted gloss or just line your lips with a red lip liner, apply clear gloss on your lips, and blend the two with your fingers.

JENNIFER LOPEZ (1969 –)

Singer, movie star, and entrepreneurial beauty mogul Jennifer Lopez started climbing her way to multi-hyphenate superstar status by dancing as one of the Fly Girls in the sketch comedy show *In Living Color* in 1992. The Puerto Rican American beauty went on to make a name for herself with her breakout film *Selena* (1997), followed by the release of her Latin-influenced pop album *On The 6* two years later. By 2001, Jennifer (who had earned the moniker "J. Lo") emerged as more than a booty-shaking diva with a bling-y image; she had become a major beauty icon for young women worldwide. And as she permeated all aspects of pop culture, so did her signature look: perfectly bronzed, glowing skin.

Suddenly, everyone was out to capture that otherworldly J. Lo glow. Though her skin was bronzed, it wasn't a look one could get at the tanning salon. Jennifer achieved her warm, glowing shine by strategically placing bronzer that refracted light on certain spots on her face, neck, shoulders—anywhere that she showed skin. With her trademark glow, which was often highlighted by her smoky eyes (see page 45) and tightly pulled-back hair, Jennifer set a new standard for UV-safe, beautiful, luminescent skin. She then used her smarts to capitalize on the craze, creating a best-selling fragrance collection and a sheen-enhancing body lotion called—what else—Glow by JLO.

Essential Jennifer

- *Selena* (film, 1997)
- *Out of Sight* (film, 1998)
- *On the 6* (album, 1999)
- *The Cell* (film, 2000)
- *J. Lo* (album, 2001)

> "You've got to have 'wow'! I tell my actress friends this all the time. I walk into auditions going, 'What's gonna make me different from all the other girls here?' They're looking for the next star to walk into that room. It's about being alive, open, electric, confident. That's the 'wow'."
>
> —Jennifer Lopez

GLOWING SKIN

WORKS BEST ON
Anyone

TOOLS NEEDED

- Highlighting concealer (one shade lighter than your foundation)
- Foundation (to match your skin tone)
- Wedge sponge
- Powder brush
- Powder bronzer

TIME IT TAKES
5 minutes or less

HOW TO GET IT

❶ With your finger, apply highlighting concealer in a strip, starting from just beneath your eyebrow arch to the outer corner of your eye. This will highlight your brow bone, and brighten your eye.

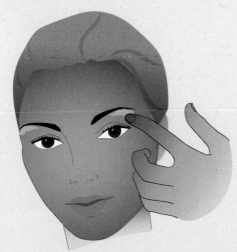

❷ Pour a quarter-sized dollop of foundation (for an average-sized face) onto your fingers. Swipe streaks of foundation across the forehead, beneath the eyes and on the cheeks, along the bridge of the nose and across the chin.

❸ With the wedge sponge, blend lines of foundation using light sweeping motions, to even out your skin tone. Blend it well, especially at the edge of your jaw so you don't see a line where your face meets your neck.

❹ Using the powder brush, lightly apply bronzer around the outer edges of your face (around your hairline, on the outer edges of your forehead, under your jawbone, and across your chin) and across the bridge of your nose and apples of your cheeks to give your face an overall glow.

Also Seen On

Lauren Conrad

Miranda Kerr

Charlize Theron

Kate Hudson

PRO TIP

If you plan to wear eye makeup with this look (a smoky eye, see page 45, looks great with glowing skin), be sure to do your eyes first; this will make the highlighting around your eyes easier.

COCO CHANEL (1883 – 1971)

Legendary French fashion designer Gabrielle Bonheur "Coco" Chanel became the queen of the industry by designing haute sportswear for forward-thinking women in the early 1900s. She was the first to introduce the little black dress as a closet staple, and her loose dress designs freed ladies of the constricting corsets of the time. But despite all of the influence she had on fashion, her most wide-reaching style contribution was bringing the look of tanned skin to the masses.

For centuries, the wealthy in Western society shunned tan skin, associating it with the poor folks of the working class who labored in the hot sun. But after the industrial revolution brought the workforce indoors, the look of the poor shifted from dark skinned to ultra-pale. Then, in 1923, Coco returned from a vacation on the Duke of Westminster's yacht in the French Riviera with a luxuriously sun-kissed tan. Suddenly, bronzed skin was associated with the rich, not the poor.

Coco's new look represented a moneyed woman of leisure who had the time to yacht about and sunbathe in tropical locales. Coco promoted the look not only on herself, but via the bronzed mannequins that displayed her clothing designs. And while the majority of people have stopped baking themselves to a crisp in fear of getting skin cancer, the tanned look still remains popular today. Now people just paint tans on with bronzers instead of soaking in the rays.

Essential Coco

- *Chanel, Chanel* (documentary, 1986)
- *Chanel: Collections and Creations* (career biography, 2007)
- *Coco Before Chanel* (biopic, 2009)
- *The Allure of Chanel* (biography, 2010)

"*Simplicity is the keynote of all true elegance.***"**
—Coco Chanel

BRONZED FACE

WORKS BEST ON
Anyone

TOOLS NEEDED

- Tinted moisturizer (in a shade that best matches your skin color)
- Angled blush brush
- Powder bronzer (use a conservative shade that complements your skin color)
- Paper towel
- Wedge sponge (optional)

TIME IT TAKES
10 minutes

HOW TO DO IT

❶ With your fingers, apply a light layer of tinted moisturizer evenly to your entire face. (If you want more of a glow, wet a wedge sponge, squeeze out excess water, and use that to apply the tinted moisturizer.)

❷ Put a bit of bronzer on the angled blush brush, then blot on a paper towel to remove any excess bronzer from the brush.

❸ Using light, sweeping motions, apply bronzer first to the edges of your face near your hairline, ears, and jawbones.

❹ Next, using light, long strokes, sweep the bronzer brush along your cheekbones and the bridge of your nose—the places where the sun would naturally kiss you. If you want to go even darker, repeat this step.

Also Seen On

Malibu Barbie
Donatella Versace
Jennifer Aniston
Gisele Bündchen

PRO TIP

Bronzed skin looks best with light makeup. Try pairing it with mascara and a red or berry lip liner and a neutral-colored lip gloss.

KATE WINSLET (1975 –)

British actress Kate Winslet shot to international stardom with her breakthrough performance in the 1997 blockbuster *Titanic*. What's notable about Kate in this movie is not just her acting (for which she received an Oscar nomination), but her naturally curvy shape, which challenged Hollywood's skinny-girl standard. Since *Titanic*, Kate has collected five other Oscar nominations, all the while keeping her healthy, curvy figure and even going nude in films like *Jude* (1996) and *The Reader* (2008).

In a similar vein, she has always kept things refreshingly real with her makeup. When not working, she has often gone bare-faced, with her hair pulled back in a simple ponytail. And even when on the red carpet, Kate has kept close to her off-duty look, wearing makeup that is made to look like she's actually makeup-free.

Kate isn't the first celebrity to wear the no-makeup makeup look—in fact, cosmetic maker Bobbi Brown pioneered this look (which seems simple, but actually requires a lot of time and products) back in the early 1990s. Kate, however, popularized the style, which is perfectly aligned with her over-all advocacy for real beauty. When the United

Kingdom edition of GQ magazine ran a cover image of midriff-bearing Kate, retouched beyond her *own* recognition and appearing 30 pounds slimmer than she really was, Kate publically spoke out against it, saying: "I do not look like that and, more importantly, I don't desire to look like that."

> **"***I've been skinny—it's f***ing boring.***"**
>
> —Kate Winslet

Essential Kate

- *Heavenly Creatures* (film, 1994)
- *Titanic* (film, 1997)
- *The Life of David Gale* (film, 2003)
- *Eternal Sunshine of the Spotless Mind* (film, 2004)
- *The Reader* (film, 2008)

NO-MAKEUP MAKEUP

WORKS BEST ON

Anyone

TOOLS NEEDED

- Foundation (in the same shade as your skin)
- Wedge sponge
- Powder brush
- Loose or pressed powder (in the same shade as your skin)
- Blush brush
- Light peachy blush
- Eye shadow fluff brush
- Eye shadow (in the same shade as your skin)
- Two crease brushes
- Eye shadow (a shade or two darker than your skin)
- Black/brown mascara
- Clear or tinted lip gloss

TIME IT TAKES

20 minutes

HOW TO DO IT

❶ Pour a quarter-sized dollop of foundation (for an average-sized face) onto your fingers. Swipe streaks of foundation across the forehead, beneath the eyes and on the cheeks, along the bridge of the nose and across the chin. With the wedge sponge, blend lines of foundation using light sweeping motions, to even out your skin tone. Blend it well, especially at the edge of your jaw so you do not see a line where your face meets your neck.

❷ Dab a bit of loose or pressed powder onto the powder brush and tap the brush to release any excess. Gently sweep the brush all over your face in long, lightly pressured motions. This will set the foundation.

❸ Put a bit of blush on the blush brush (make sure it's clean, so as not to add any extra color!), and lightly brush it on the apples of your cheeks, blending the edges as you go so as not to make any hard streaks. (If you find that the blush color is too dark, apply a hint of translucent powder to your cheeks to mute it.)

Also Seen On

Jewel
Jennifer Aniston
Uma Thurman
Natalie Portman

❹ With the eye shadow fluff brush, apply the skin-colored eye shadow to your eyelid, from your lash line all the way up to your eyebrow.

❺ With one crease brush, apply the darker-colored eye shadow only along the length of the crease line.

❻ Use the second crease brush to blend out the shadow in the crease, so that it is not a hard line.

❼ Apply mascara only to your top lashes, being careful to apply it as close to your lash line as possible. (This will eliminate the need to apply eyeliner.)

❽ Add some clear or tinted lip gloss to your lips to give shine.

PRO TIP

To make your eyes look bigger and brighter, apply a bit of foundation on your eyelid during Step 1.

KAT VON D

Renowned tattoo artist and tattoo shop owner Katherine Von Drachenberg (aka Kat Von D) found fame as a reality TV star on shows like *Miami Ink* and *LA Ink*. She came to Los Angeles from Mexico at age 7, and started drawing her own tattoos at 14. By the time she was 26 she had more than half of her body covered in ink.

But just because Kat is heavily inked doesn't mean she's let go of her girly side. She tattooed a galaxy of 21 stars on her forehead near her left eye to celebrate her femininity. The stars were inspired by the Mötley Crüe song "Starry Eyes" and, along with Kat's ruby-red lips and liquid eyeliner, give her rocker-chic look a perfectly feminine touch.

Kat may be one of the first celebrities to tattoo a face, but her look has roots in glam rock history. David Bowie painted glittery designs on his face in his 1970s Ziggy Stardust days, and Cherie Currie of '70s rock band The Runaways did the same thing.

While Kat went permanent with her starry tattoo, she could also appreciate the desire to sport an inked look on one's face for a day rather than a lifetime. So, in 2008, she launched a vintage Hollywood-meets-LA-rocker makeup line that included a tattoo liner, an eyeliner, and temporary tattoo-maker in one. Her line also includes a tattoo concealer, for those who already have tattoos that they want to hide from time to time.

SKIN & FACE

Essential Kat

- *Miami Ink* (TV series, 2005)
- *LA Ink* (TV series, 2007)
- *High Voltage Tattoo* (book, 2009)

> **"***I am a canvas of my experiences: My story is etched in lines and shading, and you can read it on my arms, my legs, my shoulders, and my stomach.***"**
>
> —Kat Von D

FACE TATTOOS

WORKS BEST ON

Lighter skin tones (darker skin tones can use white, not black, liner)

TOOLS NEEDED

- Liquid foundation
- Wedge sponge
- Powder brush
- Translucent powder (loose or pressed)
- Fine pointed liner brush
- Black liquid or gel liner

TIME IT TAKES

5 minutes

HOW TO DO IT

❶ Pour a quarter-sized dollop of foundation (for an average-sized face) onto your fingers. Swipe streaks of foundation across the forehead, beneath the eyes and on the cheeks, along the bridge of the nose and across the chin. With the wedge sponge, blend lines of foundation using light sweeping motions, to even out your skin tone. Blend it well, especially at the edge of your jaw so you do not see a line where your face meets your neck.

❷ Dab a bit of translucent powder onto the powder brush and tap the brush to release any excess. Gently sweep the brush all over your face in long, lightly pressured motions. This will set the foundation.

❸ Decide what kind of designs you'd like to draw (stars, a lightning bolt, a crescent moon, etc.).

❹ With the fine-pointed liner brush and liquid or gel liner, draw your desired designs. When drawing repetitive designs, make them larger along the border of your face and smaller as they get closer to the center of your face.

❺ Once the liner has dried, lightly dust some translucent powder over the design to set the liner.

❻ Draw a second coat of liner on the designs to ensure they are dark.

❼ If you want the design to look more like a real tattoo, lightly dust another light layer of translucent powder over the design, which will dull it slightly and make it look more like it's been perma-inked into your skin.

Also Seen On

Rainbow Brite
David Bowie
Ke$ha

PRO TIP

To steady your hand when creating a fake tattoo, use your pinky finger as an anchor, resting it on your face like a kickstand of a bicycle while you draw.

Supermodel and makeup mogul Iman had a tough climb to the top. When she first started modeling, she was a university student from Somalia who spoke five languages, yet her agent promoted her falsely as things like an "African princess" or a "village goat herder" in order to gain publicity. Iman went along with the publicity stunt, but later regretted it and became determined to change the racist landscape of the modeling industry. She went on to became one of the first black models to reach supermodel status, and a vocal one at that.

Throughout her career, Iman spoke out about the inequalities that people of color suffered in the modeling industry, not only in terms of pay, press, and overall exposure but in regard to makeup: There simply weren't any good products for darker-colored skin. Out of necessity, she created her own foundation (blending three colors together to create a shade that matched her skin tone) and became known as one of the most flawless faces in the industry.

Still, she was frustrated by the lack of makeup options for women of color. So after exiting the modeling world in 1994, Iman put her money where her mouth was and created a makeup line specifically for Black, Latina, Indian, and Asian women called Iman.

The line became an instant hot seller, and, eventually, a global beauty brand, providing skin-matching foundations, concealers, and powders to the beauty world's most overlooked demographics.

> **"** When I came to the US, the beauty message was 'America celebrates the girl next door.' Well, not only has the girl next door changed, the whole neighborhood has changed. **"**
>
> —Iman

Essential Iman

- *L.A. Story* (film, 1991)
- "Remember the Time" (Michael Jackson music video, 1992)
- *I Am Iman* (autobiography, 2001)
- *The Fashion Show* (TV, 2010)

SKIN & FACE

FLAWLESS FOUNDATION

WORKS BEST ON
Anyone

TOOLS NEEDED

- Lighter liquid foundation (the same shade as the "mask" area of your face—the area around your eyes and nose, and across your forehead)
- Darker liquid foundation (the same shade as the perimeter of your face)
- Wedge sponge
- Powder brush
- Translucent powder (loose or pressed, the same shade as "mask" area of face)

TIME IT TAKES
10 minutes

HOW TO DO IT

❶ Pour a small amount of the lighter foundation onto your fingers. Swipe streaks on the areas around your eyes and nose, on your nose, and across your forehead.

❷ Pour a small amount of the darker foundation onto your fingers. Swipe streaks along the perimeter (outer edges) of your face, and across your cheekbones and chin.

❸ Using the wedge sponge, blend the lines of the two colors of foundation together and into your skin using light sweeping motions, to even out your skin tone. Blend it well, especially at the edge of your jaw so you do not see a line where your face meets your neck.

❹ Dab a bit of translucent powder onto your powder brush and tap the brush to release any excess. Gently sweep the brush all over your face in long, lightly pressured motions. This will set the foundation.

Also Seen On

Meryl Streep

Michelle Yeoh

Zoe Saldana

PRO TIP

When deciding between pressed or loose powder, take the following into consideration. With loose powder, you can pick up just a small amount with a brush, to achieve a softer, more refined look. Pressed powder, however, offers thicker coverage and is better for hiding blemishes; because of its packaging, it's also better for touch-ups on the go.

UMA THURMAN (1970 –)

American actress Uma Thurman was named after a Hindu goddess, met the Dalai Lama at age nine, and was raised by the first American man to be ordained a Tibetan Buddhist monk. Surrounded by heavenly imagery throughout her childhood, it comes as no surprise that she became known for having an angelic look when she made her first films, *Dangerous Liaisons* (1988) and *Henry & June* (1990). In these movies, the fair-skinned Uma played naïve, airy characters and reviewers soon started labeling her as an "ethereal beauty."

But Uma felt she was being typecast, and sought out gritty roles in blockbuster action movies like *The Avengers* (1998) and *Kill Bill: Vol. 1* (2003) in an attempt to be taken more seriously. It worked, and she became known more for her diversity onscreen than for her heavenly face. Then, as she became more accomplished in her career, she began to develop a red carpet look that took on the angelic qualities she was no longer playing up on screen. This look consists of eyes brightened by iridescent shadow and luminescent skin that refracts light. Uma claims to drink gallons of spring water a day, but most of us need more than water to look like an angel. To this end, several cosmetic companies have created highlighting products that provide an angelic sheen—no Buddhist blessings required.

Essential Uma

- *Dangerous Liaisons* (film, 1988)
- *Mad Dog and Glory* (film, 1993)
- *Pulp Fiction* (film, 1994)
- *Kill Bill: Vol. 1 and Vol. 2* (films, 2003, 2004)

"*I did get pigeonholed. I started to be seen—and complimented—for my stillness in a cinematic way. If you go back, you'll see I had a lot of what I call 'corpse parts'. And I started to be referred to as 'ethereal.' Of course, I didn't feel ethereal. Nobody feels ethereal. I don't see anyone in real life as ethereal.*"

—Uma Thurman

ETHEREAL MAKEUP

WORKS BEST ON

Anyone. Those with darker skin will need less product, since darker skin tends to be oilier than lighter skin.

TOOLS NEEDED

- Liquid foundation
- Wedge sponge
- Powder brush
- Translucent powder (loose or pressed, in a shade that matches your skin)
- Angled eyeliner brush
- White, iridescent eye shadow
- White eyeliner pencil (with a blunted tip)
- Concealer brush (optional)
- Creme highlighter

TIME IT TAKES

10 minutes

HOW TO DO IT

❶ Pour a quarter-sized dollop of foundation (for an average-sized face) onto your fingers. Swipe streaks of foundation across the forehead, beneath the eyes and on the cheeks, along the bridge of the nose, and across the chin. With the wedge sponge, blend lines of foundation using light sweeping motions, to even out your skin tone. Blend it well, especially at the edge of your jaw so you do not see a line where your face meets your neck.

❷ Dab a bit of powder onto the powder brush and tap the brush to release any excess. Gently sweep the brush all over your face in long, lightly pressured motions. This will set the foundation.

PRO TIP

To avoid getting poked in the eye while lining the inner rim of your eye, dull your eyeliner pencil first by doodling on your hand before using it on your eye.

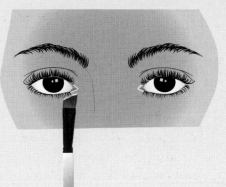

❸ Dip the angled eyeliner brush into the eye shadow and tap the brush to release any excess. Then, with a tapping motion, apply the shadow to the skin at the inner corner of your eye where your upper and lower lash line meet. Blend the color so no harsh lines appear.

❹ With the eyeliner pencil, line the inner rim (water line) of your lower eyelid from the inside corner of your eye all the way to the outside corner. (For a more dramatic look, you can also line the inner rim of your upper eyelid.) See the Pro Tip on page 49 for tips on lining the waterline.

❺ With the concealer brush or the tip of your pointer finger, apply creme highlighter to these three areas: your brow bone, the skin just above the Cupid's bow on your lip, and just above the cheekbones (but not too close to the eye). Blend the edges of the highlighter as you go so as not to create harsh lines. When using your finger, tap the product onto your skin rather than applying it in a sweeping motion.

Also Seen On

Liya Kebede
Kate Hudson
Liu Wen
Garcelle Beauvais
Blake Lively

BJÖRK (1965 –)

Offbeat singer and performer Björk has achieved phenomenal success without ever truly going mainstream. The Icelandic vocalist's songs have rarely been played on the radio in the US, but she's sold millions of albums internationally both as a frontwoman for the alternative rock band The Sugarcubes and, later, as a solo artist. Her only film appearance, in *Dancer In The Dark* (2000), was more art house than Hollywood, yet it earned her an Oscar nomination. And her influence on style has been similar: She's been alternative, to say the least, but has been nothing short of a scene stealer.

In 2001, she wore an outrageous swan-shaped, tulle dress to the prim-and-proper Academy Awards. (The press criticized the dress, but people are still talking about it.) And for her *Medulla* album in 2004, she braided her hair in a basket-weave pattern, a look that popped up on models at fashion designer Alexander McQueen's runway show six years later. Björk has also painted her forehead in tribal-inspired designs and made herself up as a geisha girl. But one of her wildest looks was a jewel-encrusted face, which she wore at the 2003 Fashion Rocks event in London. Years later, Lady Gaga did the same, using pearls to achieve the look. In the end, Björk's willingness to be a beauty renegade has inspired people worldwide to tap into their own inner oddball.

> **"** *I'm always a sucker for creativity. It wins me over every time.* **"**
>
> —Björk

Essential Björk

- **"Big Time Sensuality"** (music video, 1993)
- *Volumen* (DVD, 1999)
- *Dancer in the Dark* (film, 2000)
- *Björk* (photographic autobiography, 2001)
- *Björk's Greatest Hits* (album, 2002)

FACE ORNAMENTATION

WORKS BEST ON

Anyone

TOOLS NEEDED

- Eyelash adhesive
- Rhinestones, lace, bindis, or other adornments
- Tweezers (optional)

TIME IT TAKES

3–15 minutes depending on the design

HOW TO DO IT

❶ Apply any desired makeup.

❷ Decide what kind of decoration you'd like to wear. This can be anything lightweight and flat on one side, such as a rhinestone glued on the outside corner of the eye, a felt bindi glued on the forehead between your eyes, or a lace cutout placed off-center near your hairline. You can also create more complicated designs (like Björk did). Consider arranging your adornments in the design of a flower, star, or diamond.

❸ Sparingly apply lash adhesive to the back of the adornment or ornament. (When you press the adornment to your face, the glue will spread out.) Blow on the glue for a couple of seconds before applying. (If the glue is too wet, the rhinestone can move once placed on your face.)

❹ Apply the adornment to your face with your fingers or, if you prefer, tweezers, which can help you place the object with more precision. Repeat as necessary.

Also Seen On

Lady Gaga
Demi Moore
Gwen Stefani

DEBBIE HARRY (1945 –)

Debbie Harry came on to the music scene in the 1970s as the lead singer of the New Wave band Blondie—a name that paid tribute to her platinum peroxide hair, which was cut in a messy fringed bob. The band was certainly accomplished musically—it boasted chart-topping hits like "Heart of Glass" and "Call Me," and helped bring rap music to the mainstream with its rhyme-infused song, "Rapture." But style was also a big part of the band. Debbie hung with luminaries like designer Stephen Sprouse and artist Jean Michel Basquiat, who were stars of the New York art scene, and she rocked an edgy street style that dripped with downtown cool.

SKIN & FACE

When it came to makeup, Debbie favored bright strokes of color. She wore a sultry smoky eye with a dash of blue shadow, deep red lips that emphasized a Cupid's bow (see page 13), and brightly blushed cheeks, which played up her ultra-wide cheekbones. Her blush created a vibrant and angular look that became her makeup trademark, and was right in step with the pop art movement of the 1980s, which consisted of bold, graphic designs on clothing (like those of Sprouse, who designed clothes for her) and bright colors in paintings (like those of Basquiat, who appeared in her "Rapture" video). Before long, nightlife-loving girls across the globe were painting their faces like pop art canvases, and wearing makeup to mime her ultra-chiseled cheeks.

Essential Debbie

- *Parallel Lines* (album, 1978)
- *Autoamerican* (album, 1980)
- *Downtown 81* (film, 1981)
- *"Rapture"* (music video, 1981)
- *Making Tracks: The Rise of Blondie* (autobiography, 1998)

> **“** *Yeah, before our time … you didn't hear a lot of pop music with girls in it. It was a man's world—the good ol' boys chugging their guitars. So we were really counterculture. And urban. We were incorporating new technologies, sounds, ethnicities—just jamming it all together.* **”**
>
> —Debbie Harry

DEFINED CHEEKBONES

WORKS BEST ON
Anyone

TOOLS NEEDED

- Angled blush brush
- Warm brownish powder blush
- Powder brush
- Powder (loose or pressed, in a shade that best matches your skin color)

TIME IT TAKES
3 minutes

HOW TO DO IT

❶ Dab a bit of blush on the angled blush brush and tap the brush to release any excess. Locate the place on your face right under your cheekbones (it's the dent that is created when you suck your cheeks in). Hold the angled blush brush so the tips of the bristles touch your face head-on (rather than at an angle). Apply blush just under your cheekbone in a stroking motion going from the outer edge of your face in toward the center of your face. Repeat with continual strokes to get the desired intensity.

❷ Dab a bit of powder onto the powder brush, and tap the brush to release any excess. Apply the powder softly to the outer edges (both top and bottom) of your blush line. This will blend out the blush, and ensure you aren't left with a hard line between your blushed and unblushed skin.

Also Seen On

Faye Dunaway

Cate Blanchett

Kate Moss

PRO TIP

To create the right contour for your face, be sure to only apply blush under the cheekbone, and not on top of it.

LUCY LIU (1968 –)

In the still predominantly white Hollywood landscape, Asian-American actor Lucy Liu has become known for consistently pushing traditional racial stereotypes by playing cool, butt-kicking women in both TV (as a whipsmart, icy lawyer in *Ally McBeal*) and film (as one of the street-fighting *Charlie's Angels*). She has carved out a place for herself as a top actress—and a considerably high paid one, as well.

But despite her high visibility, Lucy is famously known for having a low-maintenance beauty routine. She is one of a rare few who has ever flaunted her freckles (even screen goddess Marlene Dietrich went to great lengths to cover hers up), and lists her must-have beauty product as Aquaphor, a skin ointment that she uses as a lip gloss and moisturizer, even though it's intended for scrapes and cuts.

Though she keeps her look fairly low key, there is one part of it that pops: her signature pinched-pink cheeks. Paired with her freckled skin, her fresh pink cheeks give Lucy's look a warm, sunny vibe. Her off-screen look is not only pretty, it serves as a reminder that beneath the hard-edged persona she's created on screen is a genuine sweetness.

SKIN & FACE

❝ *True beauty is about looking effortless.* **❞**
—Lucy Liu

Essential Lucy

- *Ally McBeal* (TV series, 1998–2002)
- *Charlie's Angels* (film, 2000)
- *Kill Bill, Vol. 1* (film, 2003)

PINCHED-PINK CHEEKS

WORKS BEST ON
Anyone

TOOLS NEEDED
• Pink, creamy blush or
  liquid stain

TIME IT TAKES
2 minutes

HOW TO DO IT
❶ Decide whether you want to use the blush
   or the liquid stain.

With the blush:

❶ With your fingers, apply the creamy blush to
   the apples of your cheeks in a small tapping,
   circular motion until you achieve the desired
   intensity. The creamy blush will create a dewy,
   fresh look. To find the apples of your cheeks,
   just smile—the apple is the round area close
   to your nose.

❷ With your fingers, blend the blush so that there
   is not a hard line between your blushed and
   un-blushed skin.

With the liquid stain:

❶ Place a few drops of stain on your index finger
   and apply to the apples of the cheeks in a small
   tapping, circular motion until you achieve the
   desired intensity. To find the apples of your
   cheeks, just smile—the apple is the round
   area close to your nose.

❷ With your middle,
   stain-free finger,
   blend the stain so
   that there is not a
   hard line between
   your blushed and
   unblushed skin.

Also
Seen
On

Chelsea Handler
Sarah Jessica Parker
Cameron Diaz

PRO TIP

*To achieve a drier, more matte
finish, replace the creamy blush
with powder blush.*

DOLLY PARTON (1946 –)

The granddaughter of a rural preacher, singer Dolly Parton emerged from a modest Tennessee upbringing to become one of country music's biggest and sexiest artists. As a singer, she's earned seven Grammys and has had more number-one hits than any other female musical artist. As an actor, she stole the show as the sassy take-no-bull secretary in the classic comedy *Nine to Five* (1980). And as a proud Smoky Mountain country girl who honors her heritage, she opened an amusement park called Dollywood, in her home state. Throughout it all, Dolly's always stayed true to her rustic roots by donning a country-girl look that she's dubbed "Backwoods Barbie." The look consists of big poufy beauty parlor hair, slinky clothes, and more-is-more makeup.

While Dolly has worn increasingly exaggerated makeup styles over the years, her original look is the one that has made beauty history: blue eye shadow to match her big, blue eyes and dusty rose cheeks brushed atop the apples of her peaches-and-cream complexion. Those warm, rosy cheeks have become a staple of the hot-to-trot, country-girl look, and iconic country women who have come after Dolly (like Daisy Duke from the TV show *The Dukes of Hazzard* and pop-crooner Jessica Simpson) have used this look as a blueprint.

Essential Dolly

- *Nine to Five* (film, 1980)
- *Steel Magnolias* (film, 1989)
- *Dolly: My Life and Other Unfinished Business* (autobiography, 1995)
- *Very Best of Dolly Parton* (album, 2007)

> *I'm not offended by all the dumb blonde jokes because I know I'm not dumb . . . and I also know that I'm not blonde.*
>
> —Dolly Parton

COUNTRY ROSE CHEEKS

WORKS BEST ON
Milky, ivory skin

TOOLS NEEDED

- Blush brush
- Soft peachy blush
- Powder (loose or pressed, in a shade that best matches your skin color—optional, see Pro Tip)
- Powder brush (optional, see Pro Tip)

TIME IT TAKES
2 minutes

HOW TO DO IT

❶ Dab a bit of blush onto the blush brush and tap the brush to release any excess. Then, dab the blush onto the apples of your cheeks. To find the apples of your cheeks, just smile— the apple is the round area close to your nose.

❷ Using a sweeping motion with your blush brush, pull blush from your apple cheeks back toward your ears. Caution: Go light on the blush, or it will result in streaks across your face.

Also Seen On

Taylor Swift
Jessica Simpson
Carrie Underwood
Reese Witherspoon

PRO TIP

This look is meant to be a bit dramatic, so you wouldn't typically blend out the blush. However, if you feel you've applied too much blush, you can blend the outer edges of the blush line. To do so, dab a bit of loose or pressed powder onto your powder brush, and apply it softly to the outer edges (both top and bottom) of your blush line.

PRO TIP

To make this a casual, daytime look, wear soft, neutral colors on the eyes. For a more dramatic evening look, wear it with a smoky eye (page 45) and light lip (pages 17 and 25).

HAIR

Scientifically speaking, healthy hair is pretty amazing stuff. It can stretch up to 30 percent of its length and can soak up its weight in water. These malleable strands that spring from our heads are practically made for styling—and we have been manipulating our tresses since the beginning of time. We make it longer, shorter, curlier, straighter, browner, redder, greener! Want sweet little ringlet curls? Take a cue from Mary Pickford (page 114). Looking for a more controlled look? Anna Wintour (page 94) gave new meaning to the bob. Ready to let your waves fly free? Diana Ross (page 102) shows us how it's done. And it's not so difficult to transform our locks, like it was back in the day. Ancient Romans covered their hair in pigeon dung as a preparation for bleaching it with ammonia, and even our more recent foremothers of the 1960s and '70s used regular clothing irons to straighten their tresses. Lucky for us, we can get the looks of the most famous hair icons in a relatively easy manner without ruining our hair. Today's innovative curlers, flat irons, and blow dryers are easier on our hair and scalps, and provide us with a myriad of ways of taking our hair from plain to playful.

BRIGITTE BARDOT (1934 –)

In 1956, French temptress Brigitte Bardot was introduced to American audiences with her film … *And God Created Woman*. In it, a bikini-clad Brigitte skipped along the streets of St. Tropez donning a sexy, pouty look. Because of the playful way she flaunted her sexuality, the press soon dubbed her a "sex kitten," an expression that soon became part of the American vernacular.

Brigitte's sex kitten look consisted of a few false lashes at the corners of her lids and a wing of black eyeliner to make her eyes look large and innocent (see pages 31 and 51); a prominent pout that was achieved by painting her lips a rich matte pink and overdrawing the outline to make them appear bigger; and her bedhead hair—long blonde tresses pumped up to epic volumes through methods of curling and teasing. Whether worn up or down, her slightly tangled, suggestive bedhead was about the flirtiest thing you could imagine, and the furthest you could get from the perfectly pinned, prudish hair of the early 1950s.

Brigitte, who went on to make movies like *A Very Private Affair* (1962) and *Contempt* (1963), not only flaunted the look in her films, but lived the part of a sexually liberated woman off screen: She had a number of well-documented affairs and, along with her bedhead, helped to set the stage for the impending sexual revolution of the 1960s.

HAIR

Essential Brigitte

- *… And God Created Woman* (film, 1956)
- *Contempt* (film, 1963)
- *Viva Maria!* (film, 1965)
- *The Best of Bardot* (album, 2005)

❝ *I am really a cat transformed into a woman… I purr. I scratch. And sometimes I bite.* **❞**

—Brigitte Bardot

BEDHEAD

WORKS BEST ON

Long hair that is straight, straightened, wavy, or relaxed

TOOLS NEEDED

- Mousse
- Blow dryer with nozzle attachment
- Large round brush
- Large-sized Velcro ceramic-lined rollers
- 1/2-inch curling iron
- Medium-hold hairspray or finishing spray
- Teasing comb (optional, see Pro Tip)

TIME IT TAKES

30 minutes

HOW TO DO IT

❶ Towel dry and comb hair, leaving it damp. If your hair is thin, apply mousse to the roots to give it some lift and volume.

❷ Turn head upside down, and blow-dry hair, finger combing through it, from the roots down to the ends.

❸ Flip your head right side up. Using the large round brush, blow-dry all of the hair on the crown of your head (the hair that covers the top three inches of your head, from root to ends) in 1-inch sections, starting with the front of your head and moving toward the back.

❹ Starting at your hairline along your forehead, wrap 2-inch sections of hair in the rollers, wrapping hair under the roller and away from the face toward the back of your head. Continue rolling hair until you've reached the back of the crown. Leave the bottom section of the hair unrolled.

❺ Using a large round brush, blow-dry the rest of your hair.

❻ Use the curling iron to curl the remaining hair. Spiral wrap 1- to 2-inch sections of hair around the barrel, leaving the ends (the last 1–2 inches of hair) uncurled.

❼ Remove rollers from Step 4 and run your fingers through the curls to break them up. It should look tousled and windblown. (If you like, pin up your hair up in a half up/half down style.)

❽ Finish with a light mist of spray.

PRO TIP

To create even more volume, backcomb (or "tease") your hair at the roots. To do this, hold a 1-inch section of hair straight up and away from your head, place your comb in your hair about an inch or two from the roots and comb toward the roots repeatedly until the desired amount of lift is achieved. Do this for as many sections as you like.

Also Seen On

Claudia Schiffer
Scarlett Johansson
Pamela Anderson
Cameron Diaz

ANNA WINTOUR (1949 –)

Anna Wintour has often been described as the most powerful woman in the fashion industry—but she's never designed a collection, owned a shop, or hand sewn a gown. Instead, Anna has wielded her influence as the long-reigning editor-in-chief of *Vogue*, championing the most talented new designers and dictating what's next for fashionistas and retailers alike. And she reigns with a notoriously iron fist, making and breaking careers with her decisive, spare-no-feelings style. In fact, the 2006 film *The Devil Wears Prada*, which is about a tyrannical editor of a fashion magazine, is allegedly based on Anna.

It's hard to say how tough Anna really is, but her signature hairstyle—a sleek, perfectly coifed bob—definitely matches her reputation. The very qualities of the cut are precise, blunt, and meticulous. Legend has it that she first got the cut at age 15 and has kept the style for more than 50 years. But the bob isn't, by its nature, the hairstyle of a perfectionist. When the look was first made famous by 1920s Jazz Age flapper girls and silent film stars like Louise Brooks, it was associated with fun party girls who wanted to trim their traditionally long and burdensome locks in the spirit of freedom and rebellion. Over the years, Anna has redefined the image of the bob to be less about anti-establishment and rebellion, and more about take-no-prisoners, queen bee chic.

> *In the face of my brothers' and sister's academic success, I felt I was rather a failure. They were super bright so I guess I worked at being decorative. Most of the time, I was hiding behind my hair and I was paralytically shy. I've always been a joke in my family. They've always thought I am deeply unserious.*
>
> —Anna Wintour

Essential Anna

- *Stylist: The Interpreters of Fashion* (style guide, 2007)
- *The September Issue* (documentary, 2009)
- *60 Minutes: Anna Wintour* (TV interview, 2009)

SLEEK BOB

WORKS BEST ON

Shoulder-length or shorter hair that is straight, straightened, wavy, or relaxed.

TOOLS NEEDED

- Medium-sized Velcro ceramic-lined rollers
- Blow dryer
- Flat iron (that heats to 400 degrees)
- Comb
- Medium-hold hairspray
- Shine spray (optional)

TIME IT TAKES

25 minutes

HOW TO DO IT

❶ Start with hair that is 85 percent dry. With the rollers, roll 1-inch sections of hair up and away from the face. Rollers should be parallel to your hairline. Roll all hair (but not the bangs). Start from the front of your hairline and go back toward the back of your head.

❷ If you have bangs, roll them in the opposite direction, under and toward your hairline.

❸ Using a high heat setting, blow-dry the hair in the rollers for 15 seconds. (This will give natural lift and body to the hair.) Then let the rollers sit for 5–10 minutes (the longer you let it sit, the more volume you'll get). Remove rollers.

❹ Comb through your hair with your fingers.

❺ Flat iron just the last ½ inch of the ends of your hair (excluding the bangs). This will create sleekness without taking away the volume you just created.

❻ Comb bangs into place.

❼ Spray a light layer of hairspray over your entire head to set your hair. You can also use a light layer of shine spray to keep it from looking dull.

Also Seen On

Isabella Blow

Christina Ricci

Josephine Baker

Edna Mode (in the cartoon The Incredibles)

Mary Quant

PRO TIP

This style makes your hair look instantly thicker so it is great for people with thinner hair.

ALI MACGRAW (1938 –)

In 1968, Ali MacGraw was a New York City career girl working as a magazine stylist and sometime model. She found her way into films just one year later, and mesmerized audiences with back-to-back onscreen portrayals of two preppy co-eds in *Goodbye, Columbus* (1969) and *Love Story* (1970). She was hailed for her onscreen charisma, but it was her look in the films—a wholesome, carefree style that consisted of barely-there makeup and long, naturally windswept hair that people still remember today.

After the films came out, Ali's look soon transcended the silver screen. Just three weeks after *Love Story*'s release, MacGraw graced the cover of *TIME* magazine with her straight hair framing her face under a banner that read "The Return to Romance." The cover sealed Mac-Graw's status as cultural icon.

Onscreen and off, Ali's center-parted, high-gloss hair was often kept tame by a peasant bandana or a knit cap (which came to be known as the "Ali cap")— a look right in stride with the bohemian hippie movement of the late 1960s. The au naturel look was feminist while still remain-

ing deeply feminine. Though her "It Girl" status faded quickly, women have continued to adopt her hairstyle ever since; its vitality, youthfulness, and ease have made it a popular style for all time.

> **“**Daddy used to see me get off the train in my model regalia and he would be so horrified that I took to scrubbing my face clean in the women's room of Grand Central Station, like some hooker with a day job at a convent. **”**
> —Ali MacGraw

Essential Ali

- *Goodbye Columbus* (film, 1969)
- *Love Story* (film, 1970)
- *The Getaway* (film, 1972)
- *Moving Pictures* (autobiography, 1991)

HAIR

96

LONG, WINDSWEPT HAIR

WORKS BEST ON

Shoulder-length or longer hair that is straight, straightened, wavy, or relaxed

TOOLS NEEDED

- Blow dryer
- Large round brush
- Strong-hold hairspray

TIME IT TAKES

15 minutes

HOW TO DO IT

❶ Start with damp hair and blow-dry hair in 2-inch sections. To do this, pick up one section at the root with the round brush while holding the dryer by the nozzle, and pull the brush down the length of your hair, moving the dryer alongside the brush.

When you reach the tips, twist the brush in a clockwise or counterclockwise direction before letting go of the section. This will give the ends a bit of volume and bounce.

❷ Spray the section with a light mist of hairspray. Repeat steps 1-2 for each section until your entire head is dry.

❸ Part your hair in the center, then run your fingers through your hair to create the look of windblown waves.

❹ Finish with a light mist of spray.

Also
Seen
On

Angie Harmon
Demi Moore
Margherita Missoni
Angelina Jolie

BETTIE PAGE (1923 – 2008)

Pinup model Bettie Page got her start modeling in New York City in 1950 by posing in homemade bikinis for amateur "camera club" photographers who shot sexy pictures of women for underground distribution. The exposure soon led to modeling work for magazine covers in national men's publications like *Wink*, *Tattler*, and *Playboy*. Soon, Hugh Hefner was calling her "the world's ultimate pinup girl." Bettie's photos may have been considered racy in the wholesome 1950s, but they certainly weren't raunchy by today's standards—she was often clothed and was usually captured giving the camera a friendly wink and a smile.

Bettie certainly garnered a reputation for her shapely figure, but not as much attention as she later got for her signature U-shaped bangs. No matter how she styled the rest of her hair—up in a ponytail or down and wavy—her thick, shiny bangs were always cleanly brushed forward, perfectly framing her face. She became so well known for her bangs that the style became known as "Bettie Page" hair.

Bettie's career only spanned seven years, from 1950–57, but her girl-next-door-meets-racy-dark-angel look has become absolutely iconic. Her likeness continues to be seen on T-shirts, in movies, and on tribute websites across the globe, and her famous bangs are still worn on rockabilly chicks and the heavily tattooed pinup models who are known as Suicide Girls.

HAIR

Essential Bettie

- *Bettie Page: Queen of Hearts!* (photographic retrospective, 1996)

- *Bettie Page: Pinup Queen* (documentary, 1998)

- *The Notorious Bettie Page* (biopic, 2005)

> "*I don't know what they mean by an icon. I never thought of myself as being that. It seems strange to me. I was just modeling, thinking of as many different poses as possible. I made more money modeling than being a secretary. I had a lot of free time. You could go back to work after an absence of a few months. I couldn't do that as a secretary.*"
>
> —Bettie Page

PINUP GIRL HAIR

WORKS BEST ON

Shoulder-length or longer hair that is straight, straightened, wavy, or relaxed and has bangs

TOOLS NEEDED

- Blow dryer
- Large round brush
- Small round brush
- 1 medium-size Velcro roller
- Large barrel curling iron
- Strong-hold hairspray
- Shine spray (optional)

TIME IT TAKES

20 minutes

HOW TO DO IT

❶ Start with damp hair. Using the large round brush, blow-dry hair on medium/high until completely dry.

❷ With the small round brush, roll your bangs under and toward your face, and dry them completely.

❸ When your bangs are dry, use the roller to curl your bangs under, toward your face. Secure roller at the hairline. Leave the roller to set while you style the rest of your hair.

❹ Starting at the front of the head, take a 2-inch section of hair and, holding the tips in your fingers, spiral-wrap your hair around the barrel of the curling iron. Do this with the clamp (if there is one) remaining closed, your hair wrapping around the outside of it. Leave the tips (about the last two inches) of hair uncurled. Hold for five seconds. Repeat in 2-inch sections until the entire head is curled.

❺ After all sections have been curled, run your fingers through the curls from root to tip to achieve a soft wavy look.

❻ Remove the roller from your bangs and comb them downward toward your face.

❼ Finish with a light mist of hairspray. Mist with shine spray, too, to create a glossy effect.

Also Seen On

Dita Von Teese

Uma Thurman in Pulp Fiction

Katy Perry

Petra Nemcova

Veronica Lake was just starting out as an actress when she was cast in the 1940 film *Forty Little Mothers*. Veronica only had a bit part, but during the filming, she had an accidental hair happening that would forever change how people viewed her. Veronica was wearing her long hair tucked behind one ear when a curl fell forward onto her face, covering an eye during a take. Director Busby Berkeley found it so seductive that he insisted she wear her hair that way, with a blonde curtain of long bangs swooping to cover one eye, for the rest of the film. Her signature look was born.

As her acting career launched, she became known for her tough-girl roles in film noir classics like *The Blue Dahlia* (1946), *This Gun For Hire* (1942), and *The Glass Key* (1942), and her hair became the most imitated style of the decade. Soon, promotional materials from Paramount were calling her hairstyle the "Detour Coiffure" and the "Peeping Pompadour."

But the style did pose one problem: It was causing a safety hazard in the factories where women worked during WWII. The workers' peek-a-boo hair kept getting caught in the machinery. In 1942, the government actually asked Veronica to change her 'do—which she did, temporarily—but women kept wearing the style. Eventually, factories had to supply hairnets to workers. The peek-a-boo hair was here to stay.

Essential Veronica

- *Sullivan's Travels* (film, 1941)
- *The Blue Dahlia* (film, 1946)
- *L.A. Confidential* (as portrayed by Kim Basinger, film, 1997)

" *I never did cheesecake like Ann Sheridan or Betty Grable. I just used my hair.* **"**

—Veronica Lake

HAIR

PEEK-A-BOO BANGS

WORKS BEST ON
Long hair that is straight, straightened, wavy, or relaxed

TOOLS NEEDED
- Setting lotion/foam or lightweight hair gel
- Comb
- Wave hair clips
- Blow dryer
- Round brush

TIME IT TAKES
30–40 minutes

HOW TO DO IT
❶ Start with damp hair and spray it with setting lotion/foam or apply gel.

❷ Part your hair on the side. Take the diagonal section of your hair that goes from your part to your ear.

❸ With the comb, push the section of hair in toward your part, making a wave, and place a clip.

❹ Continue this method to your temple.

❺ Blow-dry the rest of your hair while simultaneously brushing it smooth with a round brush. Run extra heat over the clipped waves.

❻ When the clipped section is dry, remove the clips and allow the waves to fall free. If you want to blend the waves into the rest of your hair, comb the ends of them to blend them in.

Also Seen On

Jerry Hall

Megan Fox

Jessica Rabbit in the film Who Framed Roger Rabbit

Scarlett Johansson

DIANA ROSS (1944 –)

Diana Ross grew up in the rough-and-tumble city of Detroit, and was discovered by the founder of Motown Records when she was only a teenager. In 1961, she joined the all-women soul group The Supremes and went on to become its standout member and, eventually, an international pop icon.

When Diana first joined The Supremes, black performers in the US were few in number and especially vulnerable to criticism from the public. So the band was careful to create an elegant, ladylike image that was in step with that of their conservative white counterparts who wore conventional shift dresses and bouffant hairstyles. But as The Supremes grew in popularity, they were in more of a position to set trends, rather than follow them. They started wearing sparkling, form-fitting gowns, and Diana let her hair be what it really wanted to be: curly, kinky, and voluminously beautiful.

In 1968, Diana appeared on the wildly popular *Ed Sullivan Show*, rocking an authentic black hairstyle that few dared to wear: an afro. By now, she was one of the most visible black females in America and her afro inspired legions of black women to go au naturel and embrace the "Black Is Beautiful" ethos for themselves. Later on, as a solo artist, Diana wore a big mane of long, wild, naturally curly, diva-licious hair. Her look inspired—and still inspires—people to be true to who they really are.

Essential Diana

- *Lady Sings the Blues* (album and film, 1972)
- *Mahogany* (album and film, 1975)
- *The Wiz* (film, 1978)
- *The Ultimate Collection: Diana Ross and the Supremes* (album, 1995)
- *Diana Ross: Going Back* (autobiography, 2004)

> **"** *[Beauty] means being a good person, having integrity and loyalty and being true to your work. There's power in that! Walking around being self-indulgent about prettiness—that's not important.* **"**
>
> —Diana Ross

DIVA HAIR

WORKS BEST ON

Tightly curled, kinky hair

TOOLS NEEDED

- Super moisturizing shampoo
- Oil-free deep conditioning treatment
- Wide-tooth comb
- Lightweight gel
- Moisturizing curl cream
- Long plastic hair clips
- Blow dryer with bonnet attachment
- Pick comb
- Moisturizing oil sheen spray

TIME IT TAKES

45 minutes

HOW TO DO IT

❶ Prep hair by washing with a super moisturizing shampoo and then by using a comb-through deep conditioning treatment. After combing hair through with the wide-tooth comb, allow hair to dry.

❷ Divide your hair into quadrants: top left and right, and bottom left and right (make a "+" sign on your scalp in the back of your head and divide accordingly). Put equal-sized dollops of the lightweight gel and the curl cream (enough to fully coat your hair) into your palm, and

then mix between hands. Then, one quadrant at a time, pull the product through hair strands, from the root to the ends. Stretch your curls out to achieve extra length.

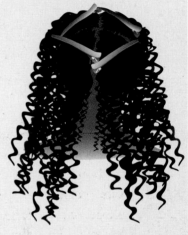

❸ Gather one quadrant together at the root, and place a plastic clip around it. Repeat on the other three quadrants. This will stretch your curls at the root, and help to elongate the hair.

❹ With the blow dryer bonnet attachment, dry hair completely on medium-high heat.

❺ Remove clips. Work a quarter-size moisturizing curl cream into hair from roots to tips, as you stretch your curls out.

❻ With the pick, pick out the hair to your desired shape and volume.

❼ Finish with a light moisturizing oil sheen spray.

PRO TIP

To keep kinky hair healthy and bouncy instead of frizzy and dry, wash every four days, and always deep condition (with heat from a hair dryer). Also, stay away from oil or oil-based products, which will weigh your hair down and clog your scalp's pores.

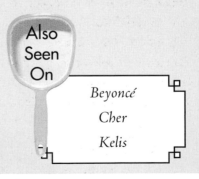

Also Seen On

Beyoncé

Cher

Kelis

DOROTHY DANDRIDGE (1922 – 1965)

Dorothy Dandridge first won over American hearts with her title performance as a sexy civilian parachute maker at an all-black army camp in *Carmen Jones* (1954). Because she played the character so convincingly, she fast developed a reputation as a sex symbol. Many saw this as a huge compliment during a time when African Americans were severely discriminated against, but Dorothy was frustrated with her reputation; she wanted to be known not as a sex symbol, but as the elegant actress that she was.

And Dorothy was certainly elegant. Her skin was perfectly powdered. Her lips were a strong and luscious red. And her hair, often set in loose pin curls struck the perfect balance of sophisticated and approachable.

Dorothy, who died at 42, had a short-lived career. But she made history as one of the first African American actors to be nominated for an Academy Award (for her role in *Carmen Jones*). And her meticulous pin curls and perfectly put-together look became a benchmark for elegance, one that women from all over continue to seek out for themselves.

HAIR

"*If I were white, I could capture the world.*"

—Dorothy Dandridge

Also Seen On

Halle Berry

Janet Jackson

Christina Aguilera

Essential Dorothy

- *Carmen Jones* (film, 1954)
- *Porgy and Bess* (film, 1959)
- *Introducing Dorothy Dandridge* (biopic, 1999)
- *Everything and Nothing: The Dorothy Dandridge Tragedy* (biography, 2000)

LOOSE PIN CURLS

WORKS BEST ON

Shoulder-length or shorter hair of all textures

TOOLS NEEDED

- Heat protectant and conditioning spray
- Blow dryer with a blow comb attachment (for kinky hair) or blow dryer with round brush (for relaxed or other types of hair)
- Flat iron (that heats to 400 degrees)
- Adjustable heat curling iron with 1-inch barrel and clamp
- Metal clips
- Alcohol-free hairspray
- Bobby pins (optional)

TIME IT TAKES

30–40 minutes

HOW TO DO IT

❶ Start with wet hair. Evenly spray entire head of hair with the heat protectant and conditioning spray.

❷ Blow-dry hair on medium/high heat. For kinky hair, hold blow dryer by the nozzle, and dry entire head of hair by "brushing" the prongs of the blow comb attachment through your hair, starting at the roots and continuing down to the tips. For relaxed or other types of hair, do the same but use a round brush instead of the blow comb attachment. Your hair (including roots) should look smooth by the time you are finished.

❸ Starting at the front of your head, take a 1-inch section of the hair and clamp it onto the curling iron at the tips. To wrap your hair around the iron, twist the iron in a counterclockwise direction, wrapping one layer of hair on top of the last so it covers a small portion of the barrel rather than its entire length. Hold till you can feel the heat on your hair. Release.

❹ Take the newly curled section, holding it at the tips, and loosely wrap it around your first two fingers. Continue to wrap hair around fingers until your fingers reach the scalp. Use a metal clip to fasten the tips of your hair to your head. Once pinned, your hair will look like a freestanding loop. Spray the loop with the hairspray and leave to set until curls are cool.

❺ Repeat steps 3 and 4 until your entire head is curled and pinned.

❻ Remove metal clips if hair is short (like Dorothy's). Simply style by arranging loose curls with your fingers. If your hair is longer, you can pin curls up with bobby pins.

❼ Finish with a light mist of spray.

FARRAH FAWCETT (1947 – 2009)

In 1976, a new TV show about three beautiful private detectives called *Charlie's Angels* catapulted three actresses into insta-fame: Farrah Fawcett, Kate Jackson, and Jaclyn Smith. The standout of this trio was Farrah Fawcett, a Texas-born actress with a supersized smile, deep tan, and angel-winged locks. At the same time the show came to the public light, so did a best-selling poster of Farrah smiling in a bright red swimsuit. The poster sold 12 million copies, and cemented Farrah as a pop culture icon. Women all over the nation flocked to hairdressers with requests of "The Farrah Do" or simply "The Farrah."

So what made this long, breezy, multilayered style so sought after? Unlike the perfectly coifed, 'dos of decades past, "The Farrah" was a casual, feathered style with tons of movement that looked as good windblown and messy as it did straight-from-the-salon.

Farrah left *Charlie's Angels* after one year to pursue more dramatic roles, including those of a domestic-abuse victim and a convicted murderer. But she'll always be remembered for her beautiful winged hair, which suggested freedom and independence: values that, in the 1970s, were in line with the women's liberation movement that was sweeping the nation.

HAIR

Essential Farrah

- *Charlie's Angels* (TV series, 1976)
- *The Burning Bed* (film, 1984)
- *The Apostle* (film, 1997)
- *My Journey with Farrah: A Story of Life, Love and Friendship* (biography, 2009)

FEATHERED HAIR

WORKS BEST ON
Shoulder-length or longer hair that is straight or relaxed

TOOLS NEEDED
- Hot rollers (preferably 1-inch)
- Hair brush
- Medium-hold hairspray or finishing spray

TIME IT TAKES
20 minutes

HOW TO DO IT

1. Start with dry hair. Heat the rollers as per product instructions. Then, starting with your hair nearest to your face, take a section of hair (approximately 1-inch, but will depend on the size of your rollers) and place the roller at the end of your hair. Roll toward your face. Continue this for your entire head, always rolling toward your face.

2. When all of your hair has been rolled, spray the rollers with the finishing spray.

3. Once the rollers are cool, unwind your hair and lightly spray again. Use your fingers to place the curls.

4. Use the brush to smooth over your hair and soften the curls.

5. Finish with a light mist of spray.

Also Seen On

Pamela Anderson

Liv Tyler

Raquel Welch

PRO TIP

To keep this look light and able to retain movement, go easy on the styling products.

> *God gave women intuition and femininity. Used properly, the combination easily jumbles the brain of any man I've ever met.*
>
> —Farrah Fawcett

MIA FARROW (1945 –)

In 1967, Mia Farrow was cast in the psychological thriller, *Rosemary's Baby*, in which she played the title role. Up until that point, Mia had been best known as the long-haired small-town sweetheart Allison MacKenzie on the nighttime TV soap opera *Peyton Place*. But during the *Rosemary's Baby* shoot, director Roman Polanski asked legendary haircutter Vidal Sassoon to visit the Paramount Pictures stage and chop off Mia Farrow's locks for the movie. Sassoon famously charged $5,000 for the cut.

Because femininity and virility had always been represented by long hair, Mia's chop was a bold move. But people loved it. The cut, dubbed the "urchin," was cropped ultra-short, and sleekly styled close to the head, which made Farrow's delicate features stand out. The new look made her the most talked about—and copied—starlet of the day.

HAIR

Essential Mia

- *Peyton Place* (TV series, 1966)
- *Rosemary's Baby* (film, 1968)
- *Hannah and Her Sisters* (film, 1986)
- *What Falls Away* (autobiography, 1997)
- *Be Kind Rewind* (film, 2008)

Over her career, Mia went on to be an accomplished actress. In the 1980s, she famously worked in a string of acclaimed films with her then romantic partner, writer-director Woody Allen. Since 2000, her acting career has been eclipsed by her work as UNICEF Goodwill Ambassador; she was even recognized by *TIME* magazine as one of 2008's most influential people for her efforts in Darfur. But fashionistas will always remember her as the one who gave daring young women license to go short, bold, and free.

> **"***I've not been dainty about experiencing life. I've absolutely plunged in. I should be fatter, really, because I eat so much.***"**
>
> —Mia Farrow

PIXIE HAIR

WORKS BEST ON
Short hair that is straight, straightened, wavy, or relaxed

TOOLS NEEDED
- Straightening balm
- Flat iron (that heats to 400 degrees)
- Medium-hold hairspray

TIME IT TAKES
5 minutes

HOW TO DO IT

❶ Start with combed, dry hair. Place a dime-sized dollop of the straightening balm in your hands, and run your fingers through your hair, smoothing out flyaways or wayward pieces.

Also Seen On

Audrey Tautou

Audrey Hepburn

Jean Seberg

Natalie Portman

Halle Berry

Emma Watson

❷ Using the flat iron, press ½-inch sections of your hair straight. Starting at the root of your hair, clamp a section into the iron, then quickly pass the iron through the length of your hair to the tip. This should be a quick, continuous motion. Do not hold the iron still at any point in this process or it will burn your hair. Repeat with a second pass through the same section of hair, then move on to the next section. Repeat with ½-inch sections until entire head is straightened.

❸ Finish with a light mist of hairspray.

PRO TIP

Looking for a more kicky 'do? When straightening your hair with a flat iron, flick your wrist up when the iron reaches the tips of your hair. This will create a slight curl at the ends and give more texture to the look. To make the look even funkier, spike your hair with pomade or gel.

FRIDA KAHLO (1907 – 1954)

Mexican artist Frida Kahlo is well known for her dreamy, colorful work that often included Mexican imagery, self-portraits, and themes of suffering (she was in physical pain most of her life due to a childhood illness followed by a trolley accident). People also remember her for her famous and tumultuous marriage to muralist Diego Rivera. But she made a huge impact on the world of fashion and beauty, as well. Her style was deeply influenced by her heritage, and she displayed it by wearing traditional native clothing, naturally thick brows, and a Mexican-influenced hairstyle: center-parted braids woven with ribbons or scarves, adorned with flowers and jewelry, and pinned up like a regal crown.

Though the public often thought her dark, ungroomed brows were too masculine and that her woven hairstyles were unfinished, Frida did eventually make the cover of *Vogue Paris* in 1938. She later became a timeless inspiration for makeup artists and fashion designers worldwide, and her look has been replicated on runways by everyone from Karl Lagerfeld to Marc Jacobs and Yves Saint Laurent. But what she is often best remembered for is the powerful, unapologetic manner in which she presented herself to the world. She didn't submit to the beauty standards of her time, but instead defined her own style—a strong, unique, and vivacious look steeped in history, boldness, and ethnic pride.

" *I paint self-portraits because I am so often alone, because I am the person I know best.* **"**

—Frida Kahlo

Essential Frida

- *Frida Kahlo: The Paintings* (photographic biography, 1993)

- *Frida's Fiestas: Recipes and Reminiscences of Life with Frida Kahlo* (cookbook, 1994)

- *Frida* (as portrayed by Salma Hayek, film, 2002)

- *The Diary of Frida Kahlo: An Intimate Self-Portrait* (autobiographical book, 2005)

- *Museo Frida Kahlo* (museum, Mexico City)

BRAIDED UPDO

WORKS BEST ON
Long hair of all textures

TOOLS NEEDED

- Tail comb (comb with a long, sharp handle)
- 2 long ribbons
- Clear rubber hair bands
- Bobby pins
- Finishing spray or hairspray

TIME IT TAKES
20–30 minutes

HOW TO DO IT

❶ Start with combed, damp hair. With the tail comb, part the hair at the center into two sections, and separate them.

❷ Start with one side. First, place a ribbon on the scalp at the crown (you can use a bobby pin to hold it in place) and then begin French braiding hair down toward the nape of the neck. As you braid, weave the ribbon through the hair. Braid until the end of the hair strands, and secure the braid with a hair band.

❸ Repeat on the other side.

❹ Cross the braids over one another and bring the ends up and across the top of the head, securing them with bobby pins on either side.

❺ Finish with a light mist of spray.

Also Seen On

Lila Downs
Sienna Miller
Rachel McAdams

SIOUXSIE SIOUX (1957 –)

Punk singer Siouxsie Sioux (pronounced "Susie Sue") started her rise to superstardom after a gutsy impromptu performance at the 1976 London Punk Festival. When an act was needed to fill a last-minute slot in the roster, Siouxsie—a young, black leather–clad punk fan who was there hanging around with The Sex Pistols and fashion designer Vivienne Westwood—rose to the occasion. With no performance experience, she got on stage and recited a 20-minute rendition of "The Lord's Prayer" followed by her own version of the Beatles hit "Twist and Shout." The selections were atypical for a punk performance, but the intent behind it—to get a rise out of the audience—was punk through and through. This was the beginning of Siouxsie's long, hellraising musical career.

Soon after the festival, Siouxsie created a band called Siouxsie and the Banshees, and became a cult favorite in the punk and Goth subcultures during the 1980s and '90s. She not only exhibited originality through her off-center music, but through her look as well. She wore exaggerated Cleopatra-like eye makeup (see page 34) in dark, witchy woman hues and spiked her dark hair to epic proportions. The anti-fashion look was daring, even menacing, but totally original. And despite Siouxsie's do-your-own-thing ethos that she proselytized to her adoring public, her fanbase copied her hair and makeup so much that she became known (quite reluctantly) as the "Godmother of Goth."

Essential Siouxsie

- *Siouxsie and the Banshees: The Authorized Biography* (biography, 2002)

- *The Best of Siouxsie & The Banshees* (album, 2002)

- *Siouxsie: Dreamshow* (DVD, 2005)

PUNK HAIR

WORKS BEST ON

Bluntly cut shoulder-length or shorter hair that is straight, straightened, or relaxed

TOOLS NEEDED

- Molding paste
- Blow dryer
- Medium-hold hairspray
- Flat iron (that heats to 400 degrees)

TIME IT TAKES

20 minutes

HOW TO DO IT

❶ Start with combed, damp hair. Work a dime-sized amount of molding paste into your hair from roots to tips.

❷ Turn your head upside down. Blow-dry hair, finger-combing through it to create the spiky shape you want at the root.

Also Seen On

Tina Turner
Robert Smith
Courtney Love

❸ Flip your head right side up. Mix a few mists of hairspray with approximately a quarter-sized (for shoulder-length hair) amount of molding paste onto your hands. Work the mixture through your hair in one-inch sections, creating jagged edges at the tips as you go along.

❹ Use the flat iron to straighten random ½-inch sections of your hair, leaving others textured and spiky.

❺ Finish with a generous application of spray.

❝*What people don't understand is when punk started it was so innocent and not aware of being looked at or being a phenomenon … You can't consciously create something that's important. It's a combination of chemistry, conditions, the environment, everything.*❞

—Siouxsie Sioux

MARY PICKFORD (1892 – 1979)

Nicknamed "America's Sweetheart," Mary Pickford was a silent-film superstar who appeared in more than 80 films in 1920 alone, and who subsequently became known, for a spell, as the most famous woman in America. Mary earned her nickname by portraying sweet and submissive characters with a wide-eyed innocence. (The nickname would later be used in the press as a term to describe box-office darlings like Meg Ryan, Julia Roberts, and Jennifer Aniston.) Part of her little girl persona was her hair, which she wore in tight, cascading ringlet curls that were partially created from locks purchased from a local whorehouse.

But while Mary played up her sweetie-pie persona onscreen, she was a savvy businesswoman off screen. She negotiated with movie studios to have creative input on her projects and to be the highest paid actress of her time. She also directed films—a rare feat for a woman in the 1920s. One of Mary's biggest accomplishments was cofounding the United Artists production company

(with fellow actor Charlie Chaplin) at a time when actors didn't dream of stepping into business roles. She also cofounded the Academy of Motion Picture Arts and Sciences (the organization that hands out the Oscars). Chaplin once said that Pickford had the best head for business in the movies. That, and one of the best heads of hair, made her one tough act to follow.

Essential Mary

- *Pollyanna* (film, 1920)
- *Pickford: The Woman Who Made Hollywood* (biography, 2007)

> *I was forced to live far beyond my years when just a child, now I have reversed the order and I intend to remain young indefinitely.*
> —Mary Pickford

RINGLET CURLS

WORKS BEST ON

Long hair that is straight, straightened, wavy, or relaxed

TOOLS NEEDED

- Blow dryer
- Thermal setting spray or medium-hold hairspray
- ½-inch barrel curling iron
- Medium-size metal clips
- Medium-hold hairspray
- Finishing spray (optional)
- Shine serum (optional, see Pro Tip)

TIME IT TAKES

30 minutes

HOW TO DO IT

❶ Start with combed, wet hair. Turn your head upside down, and blow-dry hair on medium/high heat, loosely finger-combing through it, from the roots down to the tips. This will keep any natural wave intact.

❷ Take a 1-inch section of hair and spray with thermal setting spray or hairspray. Take the sprayed section and clamp it onto the curling iron while holding the iron vertically. To wrap your hair around the iron, twist the iron in a counterclockwise direction, wrapping one layer of hair on top of the last so it covers a small portion of the barrel rather than its entire length.

❸ After releasing the section from the iron, clip the ringlet curl to your scalp, allowing the top of the curl to stand free. This will allow the curl to cool in the spiral shape. Repeat Steps 2 and 3 for entire head of hair.

❹ Lightly mist hairspray over entire head.

❺ Remove clips, letting the curls fall naturally (do not comb or finger through curls).

❻ Finish with a light mist of hairspray and/or finishing spray.

Also Seen On

Tinsley Mortimer
Shirley Temple
Taylor Swift

PRO TIP

To give your curls a loose, windblown look, flip your head upside down and apply a dime-sized amount of shine serum to the hair, and break up the curls with your fingers. Then, flip your head right side up and use your fingers to piece out the look.

NAOMI CAMPBELL (1970 –)

nglish supermodel Naomi Campbell has been ruling runways for more than 25 years. She was the first black woman to appear on the cover of *Vogue Paris* and *TIME* magazines and—along with Cindy Crawford (see page 66), Linda Evangelista, Christy Turlington, and Claudia Schiffer—became one of the first supermodels to become a mega-watt celebrity and household name. Naomi has continued to impress the public with her longevity in the ultra fickle business by modeling well into her 40s.

Though her job has required her to change hair, makeup, and wardrobe at a dizzying pace, Naomi has been wearing long, pin-straight hair as a personal style since the 1990s. But since she has naturally kinky hair, like most black women, it's a look that takes quite a bit of work. To get hair this straight and this long, women with super curly hair often undergo expensive and time-consuming treatments, which can include conditioning, straightening, and the addition of weaves or extensions. But despite the effort needed to produce the style, Naomi's sleek 'do has inspired copycats of all ethnicities, and has also offered a boon to the extension and weave industry worldwide.

> **"** *I make a lot of money and I'm worth every cent.* **"**
> —Naomi Campbell

Essential Naomi

- "Freedom! '90" (George Michael music video, 1990)
- "In The Closet" (Michael Jackson music video, 1992)
- *Unzipped* (film, 1995)
- *Girl 6* (film, 1996)
- *Naomi* (autobiography, 2001)

Also Seen On

Tyra Banks

Donatella Versace

Demi Moore

Gong Li

Leigh Lezark

PIN-STRAIGHT HAIR

WORKS BEST ON
Long hair of all textures

TOOLS NEEDED

- Anti-frizz serum
- Blow dryer with comb attachment (for kinky hair) or blow dryer and natural bristle or round brush (for other types of hair)
- Flat iron (that heats to 400 degrees)
- Antihumidity hairspray

TIME IT TAKES
10–20 minutes depending on the thickness of your hair

HOW TO DO IT

❶ Start with combed, wet hair. Towel dry. Apply a dime-sized amount of anti-frizz serum throughout your hair.

❷ Blow-dry hair on medium/high heat. For kinky hair, hold blow dryer by the nozzle, and dry entire head of hair by "brushing" the prongs of the blow comb attachment through your hair, starting at your roots and continuing down to the tips. For relaxed or other types of hair, do the same but use a natural bristle or round brush, respectively, instead of the blow comb attachment. Your hair should look fluffy and smooth by the time that you are finished.

❸ With the flat iron, press ½-inch sections of your hair straight. Starting at the root of your hair, clamp section of the hair between the iron plates, then quickly pass the iron through the length of your hair to the tip. This should be a quick, continuous motion. Do not hold the iron still at any point in this process or it will burn your hair. Do two consecutive passes through each section of hair, until entire head is straightened.

❹ Finish with a light mist of antihumidity spray.

PRO TIP

For this look, and many others, girls with kinky hair can simplify styling by getting their hair relaxed. Using a relaxer to straighten hair is a very difficult process which should always be handled by a professional. If done incorrectly, relaxers can burn your scalp and cause hair loss (even Naomi has suffered from this—she was photographed with bald spots in 2010!). Make sure your salon uses a conditioned lye relaxer—other types contain calcium hydroxide, which can lead to calcium buildup, brittleness, and hair breakage. Your stylist should also apply a deep conditioning and restructuring treatment after your hair has been relaxed.

GRACE KELLY (1929 – 1982)

Grace Kelly came to fame in the Fabulous Fifties, starring in smartly costumed, classic films like *To Catch a Thief* (1955), *High Noon* (1952), and *Dial M for Murder* (1954). No matter the role she played, the prim and proper actress lived up to her first name. She glided across the screen dressed in angelic gowns and spoke her lines with soft, controlled poise. In the course of her short six-year career, she managed to snag an Academy Award, two Golden Globes, and a place in American hearts as an elegant screen goddess during a time when many actresses were building careers as flashy sex symbols.

Grace's style consisted of chic frocks accessorized with pearls and subtle makeup that simply enhanced her natural Cupid's bow lips and baby blue eyes. She often wore her hair pulled tightly back—in a bun, pony tail, or a sleek chignon—to showcase her sharp jaw line and accent her perfectly symmetrical face. In 1955, *Women's Wear Daily* said that hers was a "'fresh type of natural glamour,'" and her look was increasingly touted by top women's magazines as the gold standard. Then, in 1956, she married Prince Rainier III of Monaco and went from screen goddess to real-life princess. Whether in evening gowns and chignons or Capri pants and ponytails, Grace's elegant style has stood the test of time.

> **"** *I don't want to dress up a picture with just my face.* **"**
> —Grace Kelly

Essential Clara

- *Rear Window* (film, 1954)
- *To Catch a Thief* (film, 1955)
- *High Society* (film, 1956)
- *Grace Kelly: The American Princess* (documentary, 1987)
- *Grace Kelly Style: Fashion for Hollywood's Princess* (style guide, 2010)

SLEEK CHIGNON

WORKS BEST ON
Shoulder-length hair that is straight, straightened, wavy, or relaxed

TOOLS NEEDED
- Volumizing mousse
- Blow dryer
- Round brush
- Hair brush (preferably boar bristle)
- Grooming cream or pomade
- Bobby pins (in a shade that matches your hair color)
- Light-hold hairspray

TIME IT TAKES
15–20 minutes

HOW TO DO IT

❶ Start with combed, towel-dried hair. Apply the mousse to your roots to give your hair some lift and volume.

❷ With the round brush, blow-dry hair on medium/high until completely dry, lifting the brush away from your roots while drying. This will smooth your hair and eliminate frizz.

❸ Brush through your hair with the hair brush.

❹ Put a dime-sized amount of grooming cream on your palms and rub them together. Then smooth the cream through your hair, from roots to ends.

❺ Pull all of your hair back at the nape of the head, smoothing hair back along the head to prevent flyaways, and twist hair upward toward the crown

in a clockwise direction, tucking wayward hairs into the twist as you go along.

❻ As you work, secure twisted hair with bobby pins, tucking pins into the edge of the twist at a downward angle, pushing them through so they're hidden beneath the twist and are secured close to the scalp.

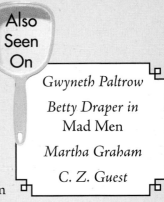

❼ Take the remaining hair that's loose at the top and tuck it into the space between the scalp and the twisted hair below. Secure with bobby pins.

❽ Finish with a light mist of spray.

INDEX

ABOUT THE AUTHOR

Erika Stalder is a California-based writer who has penned four books for teens including *Fashion 101: A Crash Course in Clothing* and *In The Driver's Seat: A Girl's Guide To Her First Car*. She writes a weekly online advice column for teens in conjunction with ABCfamily's hit show, *The Secret Life of the American Teenager*, and has contributed to various magazines including *Planet* and *Wired*. Visit her website at erikastalder.com for more on teen dating, fashion, and beauty.

AUTHOR ACKNOWLEDGMENTS

Tremendous thanks to all of *The Look Book* collaborators, including research assistants Megan Fischer-Prins and Ann Edwards, makeup artist Cameron Cohen, and hair stylist Christopher Fulton. Additional thanks to Tanya Napier, Nikki Roddy, my tireless editor Karen Macklin, and the the entire Zest Books team.

I'm grateful to everyone who answered pop culture queries, contributed ideas and grammar lessons, lent professional and moral support, and connected me with premiere beauty experts to get this book done, namely: Jeffey Baumgardner, Deborah Brosseau, Tara Green, Beth Kita, Diane Kwan, Melissa Miller, Courtney Macavinta, Eleni Nicholas, Steve-O Pavlopoulos, Rachel Shaw, Jo Stalder, Lindsay Zawid, and my Facebook fans and friends.

And to the smokin' Brian Lee: Thank you for making me happy every day.

ABOUT THE STYLISTS

Cameron Cohen is a makeup artist and brow stylist at Chroma Makeup Studio in Beverly Hills. She has also worked with makeup lines such as Bobbi Brown Cosmetics and T. Le Clerc Cosmetics, and has done makeup for stars like Miley Cyrus, Robin Williams, Hayden Panettiere, Ashton Kutcher and Amanda Bynes.

Christopher Fulton is a New York City-based celebrity hairstylist and makeup artist. Christopher has worked with countless celebrities, including Usher, Kelly Rowland, Hayden Panettiere, Kim Cattrall, and Jessica Alba. His work has appeared in Marie Claire, Vogue, Essence.com, Access Hollywood, and Vh1.

ABOUT THE ILLUSTRATOR

Ana Carolina Pesce is a Brazilian artist and graphic designer who lives in San Francisco. She has a degree in Graphic Design from University SENAC in São Paulo, and has done extensive work for various publishers in illustration, diagramming, and cover design.

Other Zest Books

START IT UP
The Complete Teen Business Guide to Turning Your Passions Into Pay
by Kenrya Rankin

QUEER
The Ultimate LGBT Guide for Teens
by Kathy Belge and Marke Bieschke

FRESHMAN
Tales of 9th Grade Obsessions, Revelations, and Other Nonsense
by Corinne Mucha

87 WAYS TO THROW A KILLER PARTY
by Melissa Daly

FASHION 101
A Crash Course in Clothing
by Erika Stalder

INDIE GIRL
From Starting a Band to Launching a Fashion Company, Nine Ways to Turn
Your Creative Talent Into Reality
by Arne Johnson and Karen Macklin

GIRL IN A FIX
Quick Beauty Solutions (and Why They Work)
by Somer Flaherty and Jen Kollmer

GIRL IN A FUNK
Quick Stress Busters (and Why They Work)
by Tanya Napier and Jen Kollmer